# Sayuri's
# Raw Dream Sweets
## Sayuri's Raw Food Cookbook Series vol. 3

# Sayuri's
# Raw Dream Sweets
## Sayuri's Raw Food Cookbook Series vol. 3

## Sayuri Tanaka

Published by PT. Benih Hayati

First published 2015

ISBN:     978-602-71673-8-4  (Paperback)
          978-602-71673-9-1 (E-book)

www.balirawchef.com
contact: tanaka.sayuri@gmail.com

Published by PT. Benih Hayati
No2 Jalan Goutama, Ubud, Bali 80571 Indonesia

Photography & Design: Sayuri Tanaka
Production: Darlene Swanson
Proofreading: Jody Amato

This book is dedicated to
those looking for the
healthiest alternatives for your family and loved ones.

This is also dedicated to someone like me who dreams
about whippy dreamy sweet cream and gets up in the
morning excited about a new creation.

I further dedicate this to all the sweets lovers who want to
fully enjoy and indulge in desserts without worrying about
gaining weight (oops! Depending how much you eat though :).

Love and gratitude,

Sayuri

2015

# Contents

# About the Author

## Sayuri Tanaka
## - Owner Sayuri Healing Food Cafe / Raw-Vegan Food Chef & Teacher

As a raw, vegan, macrobiotic chef, Sayuri offers you an experience of what it' s truly like for your body to be nourished and your heart to be opened through her food. As a teacher she shows you the simplicity of physical and spiritual transformation through the food choices we make. This knowledge has taken her around the world to share with others for over the past decades. She has catered for many yoga retreats in India, Bali, Europe, Australia, North and South America, studied at some of the great academies and learned from well-known raw food chefs. From this experiences and being a yoga practitioner herself have given her a greater understanding of preparing foods for yogis and each individual needs.

Based in Bali, the healthy lifestyle destination, her raw-vegan restaurants, "Sayuri healing food" s a leading edge of that scene, and it is continuously inspiring many visitors from all around the world. She runs "Sayuri healing food" raw food chef training regularly in Bali, where she shares her passion on sharing easily-appliable raw living food preparation for the every day life to fit into people I own individual path for the sustainable radiant healthy lifestyle combining with plant-based nutrition, ancient wisdom of Chinese Traditional medicine & Macrobiotic perspective. Through her teaching she is passionate about assisting people to find the "tool" to discover how gifted they are.

She is the author of several cookbooks. She has a magic of making could-be-intimidating raw food preparation into simple & encouraging, and she inspires the readers to discover how making food can be so much of fun, creative, and heart-nourishing.

She says, "When it comes to raw food, it s all about the flavor, texture & color! Play around it, have fun, be creative! Your excitement & inspiration & love that you put into the dish – that s the nourishment! "

www.balirawchef.com
   (retreats & raw food chef trainings)
www.sayurihealingfood.com
   (Cafe, Rawfood & Yoga classes )
www.amazon.com/author/sayuritanaka
   (cookbooks)
info@sayurihealingfood.com
FB page : Sayuri Healing Food
INSTAGRAM: sayuri_healing_food

# Foreword

Welcome to the best raw introduction! I believe it is not only myself who began a fascination with the raw food world through raw desserts and raw chocolates! In case you are already enticed by raw food and want to introduce its wonderful world to your loved ones and family, yes, raw sweets are the perfect start because they are by far more delicious, healthy, nutritious, and charged full of enzymes and love!!

How many of us have experienced regret after eating naughty sweets? Leave the feelings of guilt and heaviness and sluggishness behind! How many of us eat when we feel sad or stressed? Have you ever found relief in "eating"? Well, I have.

Yes, conventional sweets contain highly processed refined white sugar, flour, fat and salt, and pasteurized dairy, all of which make us dull and numb our senses, covering up our feelings and emotions so we do not have to feel negative emotions and pain. However, it does not cure the pain and those emotions will be stored in the body and manifested as physical ailments and disorders. Also, those foods are often full of additives and chemicals, which will be stored in the body and cause physical and mental problems.

On the contrary, raw sweets contain a full spectrum of nutrition and are abundant in antioxidants and phytonutrients, which provide a boost of energy, and happy and positive vibrations. First of all, they are by far tastier than the conventional desserts anyway! So they are the healthiest sweets choice for everyone! It's almost too good to be true that all these fancy desserts are made without animal products, wheat, and white sugar, and all the muffins and cookies are made without baking! But trust me, pinch yourself, it's not a dream. Those desserts exist. The good news is, they're also far easier to make! My favorite thing about raw sweets is you can make them by feel, whereas traditional pastry making is very strict about every single gram.

All the recipes in this book are dairy-, wheat- and white-sugar free! Perfect for those who want to avoid gluten and lactose.

Enough said! We have saying in Japan, "Seeing is believing". In this case, I would say, "tasting is believing", —all you need to do is to try a bite. You will see what I'm talking about!

# My Sweets Journey

Among all my friends, I am well known for my sweet tooth. Yes, I can easily live on sweets unless someone keeps an eye on me!

My mother introduced me the joy of cooking when I was a kid. Not long after that I started making cookies and cakes on my own and was literally finishing up the whole tray of baking desserts on my own. Not that long after, I started sharing with friends. After school, all my friends came to my place waiting for my cookies and cakes to be ready. I never gained weight, no matter how much dessert I ate, until I had to stop club activities to study for high school. That was when I switch my interest to "healthy" desserts. I started making tofu desserts and whole-grain baked goods without dairy and white sugar. The beginning seemed to be good, but at that time all my interest was about calories. I wanted to eat delicious sweets but did not want to gain weight. So I started getting into low-sugar, low-fat, low-calorie sweets that I believed were the healthiest options. I tried all the sugar alternatives available at that time, which I look back on now as the worst choices, such as aspartame and vegan margarines.

As a result, all those chemicals made me out of balance, of course. I became terrified to eat normal sweets. I could not even touch the hearty kind of grandma-made sugary desserts. Then somehow, my extremely "healthy" desserts became my escape.

I filled my loneliness and sadness, anxiety and unfulfilled-ness ⋯ all my negative emotions with that food⋯.

So it was revolutionary when I discovered macrobiotics. How fascinating to know that the food we eat reflects on who and how we are and what we think. I understood on a deep level that it actually reflects on everything happening around us. I thought how beautiful it was creating peace and harmony by eating organic, local, seasonal food and balancing our physical and mental states by choosing the constitution of the universal energy of the food. I grasped the potential of food to heal others and myself.

For me, who was brought up with the SAD (Standard American Diet), suddenly everything started making sense. It even changed my way of seeing things. It also changed my whole attitude of "eating," and I started regaining the joy of eating and sharing that I had been missing so long. What most hooked me were the vegan macrobiotic desserts. Making all the delicious, earthy, grounding goodies was so nurturing and made me feel content. I felt more nourished by sharing and by eating consciously with appreciation. I started exchanging the energy of love by making food for people and by sharing it with others. Suddenly love within started circulating again. Then everything else started flowing.

When I began travelling, people started introducing me to "raw food." When I found "raw sweets," that was it! They were the healthy choices I had been searching for for a long, long time. All the joy, happiness, deliciousness, and sensations were the next level. Although vegan macrobiotic sweets were delicious, grounding, and nurturing, raw vegan sweets were absolutely amazing, uplifting, more expressional and sensational, and completely guilt-free!

We eat energy. And we exchange the energy of love though food. If "you are what you eat," I want to become the love that I eat. I want to become the solid, flowing, shining, and endless love within by eating healthy, nutritious, vibrational food.I am still on the journey, learning myself. Each experience is precious to further understand myself—the journey of finding the true love within. And I know it is my karma to learn that through my food!

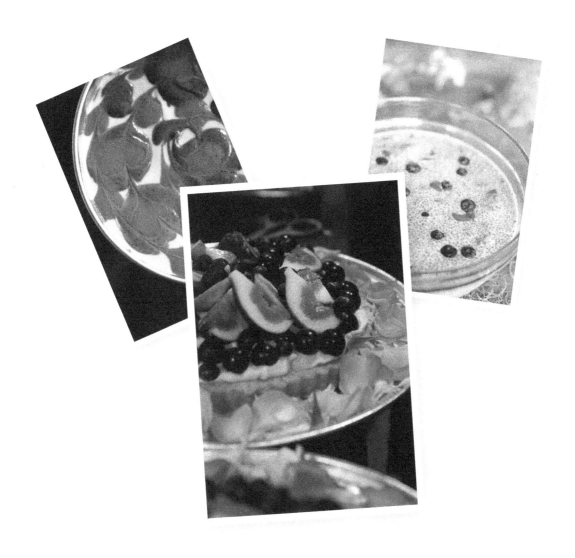

# Important Notes Before Starting

## Basic Measurement Standards

1 cup = 250ml

½ cup = 125ml

¼ cup = 60ml = 4 tablespoons

1 tablespoon = 15ml

1 teaspoon = 5ml

1 oz. by weight = 30 grams

1 inch = 2.54 cm

FYI: Ounces (oz.) are measured by weight, not by volume. When measured by volume, it is noted as such.

FYI: Measurement of nuts and seeds are before soaking. When you measure after soaking, measure 1.2-2 times more, as it increases the volume (see the soaking and sprouting time chart in the Techniques chapter for the yield after soaking for nuts and seeds. (see page 26 in the soaking and sprouting time chart in the Techniques and Advance Preparation chapter for the yield after soaking for nuts and seeds.)

FYI: When the recipe calls for dry nuts (without the instruction of soaking) I recommend the nuts and seeds be soaked and dehydrated for their health benefits.

# TOOLS FOR RAW SWEETS

## ■ Gadgets

**High-power blender:** I like the Vitamix and Blendtec brands. Most of the raw sweets recipes require the blender. A high-power blender makes your desserts super silky, with a creamy texture, and absolutely delicious!

Blendtec

Vitamix

**Food processer:** I like to use Cuisinart, Kitchen Aid or Robot-Coupe brands, but you can start with less expensive ones! It is useful to make crusts and bliss balls.

Food Processor

**Dehydrator:** I like the Excalibur and Sedona brands. It is useful to dry the activated nuts and seeds to make cookies, muffins, and to make your own dried fruits and recycle the cakes into cookies or puddings into sweet crackers! If you don't have one, don't worry; there are many recipes that don' t require it, and you can start making delicious pies, cheesecakes, and cakes all without a dehydrator! Don't forget to purchase nonstick sheets, because they usually don't come with the dehydrator.

Dehydrator

## ■ Basic Tools

Knives and cutting boards

Rubber spatulas and offset spatulas

Mixing bowls and strainers

Measuring cups, measuring spoons, scale

Whisk

Grater or micro plane

Nut milk bag or cheesecloth to make nut milk

Hand citrus juicer

Offset Spatulas

Rubber Spatulas

Measuring Spoons

Nut Milk Bag

Measuring Cup

Micro Plane

Loose-bottom pan
for Tiramisu

Spring-form pan

Loose-bottom
tart/pie pan

Silicon mini-muffin
mold

8-9 inch/21-23cm Loose-bottom cake pans

9 inch/23cm Loose-bottom pie/tart pans

9.5x9.5 inches/24x24cm square container for tiramisu
(ideally loose bottom)

Chocolate molds

Chocolate molds or ice-cube trays for chocolate

Silicon mini-muffin molds for muffins (silicon works better)

7x4 inch/18x10cm silicon pound cake mold (silicon works better)

Piping bag &
nozzles

Piping bags and nozzles to decorate the cakes

## ■ Nice to Have

Ice cream maker: I like Cuisinart and Panasonic home-size
makers. It is useful to create the smooth creamy ice cream.

Thermometer for tempering chocolate

Cleaver for opening coconuts if you are using fresh coconut

Ice-Cream maker

## ■ Where to Find the Equipment

All the equipment and tools: www.amazon.com or any amazon website close to your country

Blenders, juicers, dehydrator comparison charts, discount appliances: www.discoutjuicers.com

Vitamix blender: www.vitamix.com

Blendtec blender: www.blendtec.com

Cuisinart (food processors, ice cream makers): www.cuisinart.com

Tribest (Sedona dehydrator, Green Star and Solostar juicers): www.tribest.com

Excalibur dehydrator: www.excaliburdehydrator.com

# Ingredients: Staple and Raw Alternatives

## Raw Alternatives

This chart shows how to replace ingredients to make it into a raw dessert. Using the chart, you can create new raw sweets from the old typical dessert cookbook. Indeed, I often use that trick for inspiration for new creations.

| Traditional Dessert | Raw Dessert |
|---|---|
| Wheat flour | Nut pulp (the remains after squeezing milk), nut flour (dried and powdered nut pulp), and ground nuts |
| Milk and cream | Nuts and seeds |
| Butter | Coconut oil, cacao butter, avocado, nuts, and seeds |
| White sugar | Honey, dates, fruits (see page 19 in the Characteristics of Each Ingredient chapter for more alternatives) |
| Gelatin | Irish moss |
| Egg | Flaxseeds, chia seeds, psyllium husk, lecithin |

## Ingredient Alternatives

If some ingredients are unavailable or hard to find, try replacing them with ingredients you are familiar with that grow locally where you live. Here are some examples of substitutions:

| Ingredients | Alternatives |
|---|---|
| Young coconut meat for cream | Cashew nuts |
| Cashew nuts for cream | Macadamia nuts, pine nuts, hazelnuts, Brazilian nuts, young coconut meat |
| Nuts for milk, cookies and cakes, tart crust, and bliss ball | Any nuts and seeds |
| Dates for tart crust and bliss ball | Any dried fruit |
| Dates as a sweetener for cream | Any sweetener |
| Lecithin | Can do without |
| Coconut oil | Cacao butter |
| Flaxseeds | Chia seeds, psyllium husk |
| ½ cup Irish moss paste | ½ teaspoon agar powder (or 1 teaspoon flakes) melted in ½ cup boiled water |

## ◼ Basic Staples

Because the process of making raw sweets is so simple, the finished products depend on the quality of the ingredients used. So it is important to resource organic, quality ingredients whenever possible.

**Nuts and seeds:** almonds, Brazilian nuts, cashew nuts, desiccated coconuts(see FYI below) , macadamia nuts, pine nuts, walnuts, pumpkin seeds, sunflower seeds, hemp seeds, sesame seeds, chia seeds, flaxseeds, nut flour (see technique chapter & FYI below)

> **FYI on desiccated coconuts:** desiccated "shredded" coconut is used in this book. "Shredded" coconut is about 75g per 1 cup whereas "fine" (powder) coconut is about 100g per 1 cup, so use weight (g) measurement if you are using "fine" (powder) coconut.

> **FYI on Nut Flour:** although you can purchase ready-made "coconut flour" , I am using homemade nut flour in this book. Store-bought & homemade coconut flour is quite different in weight, so I am using volume (ml & cups) for the measurement, although it is still slightly different. If you are using store-bought coconut flour, use less amount, about 90% in volume (ml).

**Dried fruits:** apricots, cranberries, dates, figs, goji berries, raisins

**Oils and butters:** nut butter (almond, coconut, etc.), tahini, cacao butter, coconut oil

**Sweeteners:** coconut sugar (powder or liquid/syrup), dates, honey, maple syrup, unrefined cane sugar, yacon (powder or liquid/syrup), lucuma (powder), mesquite (powder or liquid/syrup), stevia (powder or liquid). (<u>See page 19</u> for more details and photos in the Characteristics of Each Ingredient chapter)

**Spices:** chili, cinnamon, nutmeg, cardamom, cloves

**Thickeners and binders:** Irish moss, psyllium husk, lecithin, chia seeds, flaxseeds, coconut oil, cacao butter (<u>See page 19</u> for more details and photos in the Characteristics of Each Ingredient chapter)

**Superfoods:** maca, bee pollen, spirulina, hemp seeds, chia seeds, goji berries, acai berry, maqui berry, cacao (powder, paste, nibs, beans, butter)

## Flavorings: (see FYI below)

**Natural flavor extracts:** vanilla, almond, and hazelnut

**"Medicine flower" flavor extracts:** rum, coffee, peanut, cherry, caramel

**High-quality pure essential oils:** orange, lemon, mint, lavender

**Dried flowers:** rose, lavender

FYI: Flavor Extracts and Essential Oils
(www.medicineflower.com/flavorextracts.html)

## ■ Where to Find Kitchen Staples

www.iherb.com or any iherb website close to your country

www.amazon.com or any amazon website close to your country

navitasnaturals.com (raw nuts and seeds, superfoods)

www.rawguru.com (raw nuts and seeds, superfoods)

www.frontiercoop.com (bulk herbs, spices, teas)

www.medicineflower.com/flavorextracts.html (medicine flower flavor extract)

www.doterra.com, www.youngliving.com (essential oils)

### FYI: Flavor Extracts and Essential Oils

1 teaspoon flavor extract can be replaced by a few drops of essential oil. However, "medicine flower flavor extract" (www.medicineflower.com/flavorextracts.html ) is extremely concentrated, so use the quantity just like an essential oil. You need just a few drops! They are organic without any coloring, additives, and preservatives and cold-pressed under 118 ° F/48 ° C. It is extremely concentrated (30 to70 times more than the normal extract) so 1-5 drops is equivalent to 1 teaspoon of normal extract. Note that its butterscotch and caramel flavors are extracted from organic creams and sugars, so it is not technically vegan; coffee is extracted from the roasted bean so it is not technically raw.

Essential oils are the oils extracted from the plant; they contain certain therapeutic properties, which have been used to promote health and well-being. For culinary purposes, choose high quality, pure organic brands such as doterra (www.doterra.com) and young living (www.youngliving.com). One tablespoon lemon or orange zest can be replaced by 2-3 drops of essential oil.

# Characteristics of Each Ingredient

The key in creating raw desserts is to be familiar with the unique characteristics of each sweetener, binder, and thickener.

## ■ Sweeteners:

Maple syrup, coconut sugar, and unrefined cane sugars are most often not raw, but each has its own health benefits and nutritional value. Depending on your need, the availability and accessibility, be flexible in choosing the sweetener. You can always use the sweetener of your choice in any recipe. Each sweetener has different characters and flavor. Note that honey does not dry, so you may want to use date paste or maple syrup when dehydrating if you are looking for a crunchy outcome. Use honey if you want your breads or cookies to come out soft.

**Raw honey** is highly nutritious and has amazing medicinal and healing properties. Although honey is not considered vegan, I use it in this book for its benefits.

**Dates** are great whole raw sweetener. It is useful to have date paste at hand. (See page 31 in the Techniques and Advance Preparation chapter for how to make date paste.)

**Coconut nectar (liquid form) & Coconut sugar (granule form)** is made from the sap or nectar from the coconut palm tree flower. If using granule form, it is useful to make into liquid so that you can replace with any liquid sugar such as honey and maple syrup etc. (See page 31 in the Techniques and Advance Preparation chapter for how to make liquid coconut sugar.)

**FYI:** Palm sugar is made from the sap of the date palm or sugar palm tree. The term is often used interchangeably with coconut sugar

**Maple syrup** is made from the sap of the sugar maple tree. It is easy to dry and crystalize, so it is one of the best choice for dehydration.

**Yacon** (powder or liquid/syrup) is a tuber native to the Andes in South America. It is low on the glycemic index, and has a dark brown, rich, molasses-like flavor.

**Mesquite powder** is ground seedpods of the mesquite plant. It is delicious for desserts and adds a sweet, smoky, caramel-like flavor. It's also a low glycemic-index sweetener.

**Lucuma powder** is a fruit native to Peru. It is a relatively low glycemic-index sweetener, and has a rich, creamy texture and maple-like flavor. It's great for ice cream as well as smoothies.

**Stevia** is an herb native to South America. Stevioside, the natural sweetener extracted from the leaves, has 300 times the sweetness of sugar, but it has zero sugar and therefore is not on the glycemic index. Due to its high concentration of sweetness, it is easy to overdo, which gives food a slight bitterness. A few drops of stevia will do for 1 portion of smoothies.

## ■ Thickeners and Binders:

**Irish moss** is not a moss, but a seaweed. It is a wonderful raw vegan alternative to animal-derived gelatin to make creams and mousses. It makes desserts healthier and lighter with less oil. It is also a great addition for smoothies, dressings, and soups to create the desired consistency.

FYI: If Irish moss is not available, though not raw, it can be substituted with agar. (See page 16 for the "Ingredient Alternatives Chart" in the Staple Ingredients and Raw Alternatives chapter.)

**Psyllium husk** is a powder that comes from the husk of the psyllium seed and is usually used as a bowel cleanser. For culinary purposes, it is used as a thickener for puddings or to make wraps. It is a great alternative thicker/binder to flaxseeds or chia seeds in case you want to make wraps without seeds.

**Lecithin** is used as an emulsifier between oil and water, such as for mayonnaise, milk, and cream. Soy lecithin is the extract from soy oil. Sunflower seed lecithin is also available.

**Ground chia seeds and flaxseeds** are useful for tart crusts, cakes and crackers, and breads to keep them held together.

**Coconut oil** is used for desserts such as cheesecakes, tarts, and cakes to solidify in the fridge. It melts at 76° F/24° C so the dessert will melt at room temperature if you are in a tropical climate.

**Cacao butter** is also used to solidify desserts. It has a higher melting point of 93-100° F/34-38° C compared to coconut oil.

# TECHNIQUES
# AND ADVANCE
# PREPARATION

# Basic Nut Milk and Variations

The basic ratio is 1:4 for nuts:water; it can be less or more water depending on the consistency you want to achieve. It is not necessary to strain some nuts such as hemp seeds, cashew nuts, or pine nuts, as they are very soft and not much pulp remains; therefore I do 1:5 for nuts:water. Because desiccated coconut is hard and has more fiber, the ideal ratio is 1:2-3 for nuts:water. You may want to soak desiccated coconut in water for 30 minutes and use slightly warm water if you are in a cold climate, as fat becomes solid in cold water.

Yields 3 cups
blender needed

1   cup nuts or seeds of your choice
4   cups water

1.  Rinse 1 cup nuts or seeds and soak in plenty of water. Soaking durations vary. (See page 27 foe the "Soaking and Sprouting Times Chart" in this chapter.)
2.  After soaking, strain and rinse thoroughly.
3.  Blend them with the desired amount of water in a high-power blender until the nuts or seeds are completely broken down.
4.  Strain through a nut milk bag or cheesecloth.
5.  It will last several days in the refrigerator.
6.  If desired, follow the directions below for variations to enrich and flavor your milk.

Variations: Here are some quick tricks and variations!

**Quick nut milk:** if you are too busy to soak nuts or want it right now, you can use nut butter. Just blend 2 tablespoons nut butter of your choice and 2 cups water together. No need to strain.

**Sweet milk:** if you want your milk a bit sweet, add pinch of salt, 1 date or ½-1 tablespoon sweetener of your choice and 1 teaspoon vanilla extract to blend with the nut milk.

**Creamy milk:** if you want it creamy, add 1 tablespoon coconut oil and 1 tablespoon lecithin to blend with the nut milk.

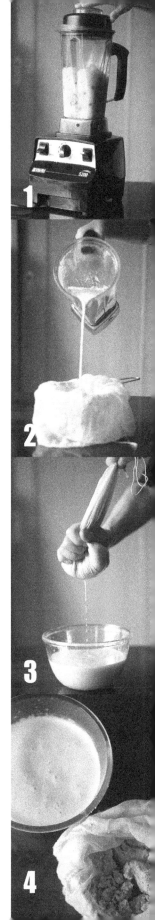

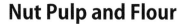

FYI on Nut Flour: although you can purchase ready-made "coconut flour", I am using homemade nut flour in this book. Store-bought & homemade coconut flour are quite different in weight, so I am using volume (ml & cups) for the measurement, although it is still slightly different. If you are using store-bought coconut flour, use less amount, about 90% in volume (ml).

# Nut Pulp and Flour

**Pulp:** Nut and seed pulps are the remains after squeezing the nut or seed milk. Store in the freezer. It will last up to 3 months. It is useful for cakes, breads, and crackers.

**Flour:** When nut or seed pulp is dehydrated until completely dry, and then ground into powder in a blender or coffee grinder, it is called "nut or seed flour." It will last up to 3 months. It' s a great flour alternative for cookies and cakes!!

FYI: The difference between pulp and flour is whether wet or dry, and also pulp is coarse whereas flour is finer. So if you like your cakes to be smoother, you might want to use flour. You just need to add some water to adjust the consistency when you are using flour for the recipes that require pulp.

Flour is a finer powder than pulp so it is ideal for cookies and cakes as a "flour" substitute, though it is totally fine to use pulp if you don' t have time to dehydrate. Just make sure to adjust the recipe to use less liquid (whether it is water or coconut oil or sweetener)

# Grinding Almonds, Other Nuts, and Flaxseeds

Ground almonds (and other nuts) are often used in desserts. Ground flaxseeds are the basic binder for crackers, breads, doughnuts, and cakes.

1. Grind in a coffee grinder or blender.
2. If you are using blender, start on the highest speed and blend no more than 1-2 cups to avoid clogging on the bottom; otherwise it becomes a paste rather than powder..
3. Once it is ground, flaxseeds easily turn rancid, so it is best to buy the whole seeds and grind them each time. In case there are leftovers, store flaxseeds in the freezer to avoid oxidation. Ground almonds are fine to store in the fridge.

FYI:
⅘ cup almond yields 1 cup ground almonds

¾ cup flaxseeds yields 1 cup ground flaxseeds

FYI: If you are grinding softer nuts and seeds such as cashew nuts, do not overblend, as they'll easily turn into a paste.

## Soaking and Activating Nuts and Seeds

We want to have our nuts and seeds activated, meaning that enzymes are awakened and they have the full potential to be beneficial for us! It is not only raw but a living food! To activate them, we need to remove the enzyme inhibitor, which is preventing them from germinating. By soaking them, they are activated so that they are ready to germinate in a certain environment. When the plants start to geminate, it causes the ammonium power to grow, and the amount of life force, enzymes, and nutrition are increased by nature. It also makes all the nutrients easier to be digested and assimilated as the complex compounds are broken down into simple forms by enzymes. Note that some cookbooks refer to activated nuts and seeds as being soaked and dehydrated. Here in this book, I use the term "activated" whether only soaked or soaked and dehydrated.

FYI: Flaxseeds, chia seeds, dry coconut, and hemp seeds do not require soaking.

# How to Soak

1. Rinse well and soak them in plenty of water. Soaking durations vary. Small nuts and seeds, such as sesame seeds, require only a few hours to soak, while larger nuts such as almonds require longer, about 8-12 hours. (See the "Soaking and Sprouting Time Chart" on page 27.)

2. After soaking, strain and wash thoroughly. They are now ready to use for the recipes calling for "soaked" nuts or seeds.

3. When you want them crunchy, dehydrate them on the mesh screen in the dehydrator until completely dry. They' re ready for snacking or use in some recipes, such as tart crusts and bliss balls.

   **Important note:** in this book, when the recipe calls for soaking, it means nuts are measured first then soaked for a certain number of hours. In case you are measuring after soaking, you need to have 1.2-2 times in quantity, as most of them swell by soaking (see page 27 for the "Soaking and Sprouting Time Chart" for the yield after soaking).

   **Important note:** using dry nuts and seeds
   When the recipes don' t mention soaking—for example, when you need them in dry form for tart crusts, crumbles, or bliss balls, I recommend the nuts and seeds (except for flaxseeds, chia seeds, desiccated coconut, and hemp seeds) be soaked and dehydrated (activated!) for their health benefits.

# Soaking and Sprouting Times Chart

| Nuts and seeds | Soaking hours | yield |
|---|---|---|
| Almond | 8-12 hours | 1 cup dry yields 1½ cups |
| Brazilian nuts | No soaking or 2-4 hours | 1 cup dry yields 1 cup |
| Cashew nuts | 2-4 hours | 1 cup dry yields 1½ cups |
| Hazelnuts | 4-8 hours | 1 cup dry yields 1 cup |
| Macadamia nuts | No soaking or 2-4 hours | 1 cup dry yields 1 cup |
| Pecans | 8-12 hours | 1 cup dry yields 1½ cups |
| Pine nuts | No soaking or 2-4 hours | 1 cup dry yields 1¼ cups |
| Walnuts | 8-12 hours | 1 cup dry yields 1½ cups |
| Pumpkin seeds | 6 hours | 1 cup dry yields 2 cups |
| Sesame seeds, hulled | 8 hours | 1 cup dry yields 1½ cups |
| Sesame seeds, unhulled | 4-6 hours | 1 cup dry yields 1 cup |
| Sunflower seeds, hulled | 6-8 hours | 1 cup dry yields 2 cups |

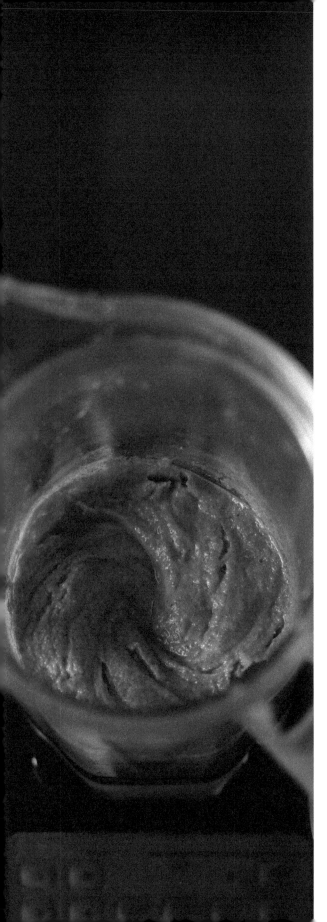

# Homemade Nut Butter

Nut and seed butters are expensive! If you have a high-power blender, you can make them at home!

## How to Make Nut and Seed Butters

1. First, we use dry activated nuts and seeds. That means they are soaked and dehydrated until crunchy. (See "Soaking and Activating Nuts and Seeds" on page 27)

2. **If you are using a Blendtec blender:** Place the nuts and/or seeds and a pinch of salt into the twister jar (see FYI on page 29), run on high speed, turning the lid with tines counterclockwise while blending. It should take only about 40 seconds.

3. You can use this technique for all nuts and seeds.

4. **If you are using a Vitamix blender:** For almond butter, as it has less oil content, it is easier to make if you add 4 tablespoons of oil (coconut oil or olive oil or unroasted sesame oil, depending on the purpose of usage).

5. Place 3 cups almonds, a pinch of salt and 4 tablespoons of oil into the blender jug, blend on the highest speed, press the ingredients into the blades using the tamper (see FYI on page 29) while blending, for about 1 minute. (Do not overprocess more than 1 minute, as it causes overheating of the machine as well as the ingredients.). Pry away almonds stuck to the bottom and sides of the container using a chopstick or fork.

6. Then blend on slow speed, pressing almonds with the tamper, for 1 minute. (In case the machine and ingredients are becoming too hot at this stage, let it rest for 20-30 minutes and start again).

7. Then blend on high speed again for 1 minute, pressing almonds down with the tamper.

8. For high-oil-content nuts and seeds such as walnuts, pecans, macadamia nuts, pine nuts, and Brazilian nuts, there is no need to add oil, but if it is difficult, add a little oil to facilitate easy blending.

9. For coconut butter, blend around 7-9 cups of dry coconut in 1 batch for easy blending. If it is difficult, add a little coconut oil to facilitate easy blending.

**FYI:** The Blendtec twister jar is designed to blend the thickest ingredients, such as nut butters and raw cheeses. It has tines along inside of the jar, which rotate and push ingredients off the side into the blending vortex.

The Vitamix tamper allows for blending thick, dense ingredients. It allows food to be pushed down into the blades without coming in contact with the blade.

# Irish Moss Paste

Rinse the Irish moss very well in cold running water.

Then soak it in a bowl with cold water, changing the water a few times until the water is clear.

Soak the moss in plenty of cold water for 3-4 hours at room temperature or 8 hours in the fridge.

Rinse and drain. It is ready to use for recipes that call for "soaked Irish moss."

When a recipe calls for " Irish moss paste," blend one cup of soaked Irish moss with ½ cup of water (see FYI on page 31) in a high-power blender until it' s completely dissolved and slightly warm. It may take a few minutes. It is ready to use once it becomes gelatinous.

Stored in the fridge, it will last more than 1 week.

> **FYI:** Adjust the quantity of water depending on the thickness and hardness of the Irish moss. Ideally, use minimum water to make a nice and thick paste.

## Date Paste

Soak pitted dates in water just barely covering the dates for 30 minutes or until they soften.

Process the dates and liquid together in the food processor or blender into a puree. Add only a little water if necessary to facilitate easy processing.

It will last in the fridge for 1 week.

## Liquid Sweetener (Liquid Natural Sugar Syrup)

Blend 1 cup granule or powder sugar of your choice (such as coconut sugar or cane sugar) with ⅓ cup water until completely dissolved in a blender.

It can be stored in the refrigerator for more than 1 month. You can use these syrups when a recipe requires liquid sweetener.

FYI: If Irish moss is not available, though it is not going to be completely raw, it can be substituted with agar.

½ cup Irish moss paste can be replaced with ½ teaspoon agar powder (or 1 agar flake) melted in ½ cup boiled water..

# BREAKFAST FOR A SWEET TOOTH

Are you looking for some variety to keep you excited about raw food, especially breakfast? This is the chapter for you :)

# Maple Banana Pancakes

I am in love with pancakes! Even more with raw banana pancakes! Sweet maple aroma coming out from the dehydrator is so irresistible. You will be dreaming of it the night before. Worth waiting for a night!

Serves 6                                                            blender and dehydrator needed

## Pancakes:

3    cups chopped bananas

1    cup walnuts (120g), soaked

1    cup cashew nuts (130g) , soaked

2    tablespoons maple syrup

1    teaspoon vanilla extract

½    teaspoon salt

1    cup water

## Assembly:

3-4   bananas, sliced

1½   cups blueberry jam (see page 50 in the Sweet Creams and Sauces chapter)

2     cups vanilla whippy cream (see page 50 in the Sweet Creams and Sauces chapter)

1. Blend all ingredients until smooth.
2. Spread ¼ cup of the mixture onto nonstick sheets and form into a 5 inch/13cm diameter circle with offset spatula. (It should make 12 pancakes).
3. Dehydrate at 105-115° F/41-46° C for about 6 hours or until dry on top, then flip it onto the mesh screen and continue to dehydrate for a few hours or until completely dry but still pliable.
4. To assemble, place 1 pancake on the plate. Spread 4 tablespoons vanilla whippy cream, fill with sliced bananas and 3 tablespoons blueberry jam over the cream, then cover with another pancake on top.
5. Decorate with 1-2 tablespoons vanilla whippy cream and 1 tablespoon jam on top.

# Chocolate Muffins with Lemon Icing

Let's get into serious business! Nutrient-dense raw chocolate meets rich and creamy icing! I promise this will be a huge hit for your family!

Yields 12 of 2 inch/5cm mini muffins
mini silicon muffin mold (see FYI on page 36 Carrot Muffins in this chapter),
blender and dehydrator needed

3   cups any nut pulp (the remains after squeezing milk). (See page 23 in the Techniques and Advance Preparation chapter)

1½  cups (225g) almond powder (ground almond) (See page 25 Techniques and Advance Preparation chapter for grinding)

¾   cup cacao powder

¾   cup date paste (See page 31 Techniques and Advance Preparation chapter)

½   cup coconut oil, melted if solid

1   teaspoon vanilla extract

½   teaspoon salt

6   tablespoons water

**Garnish:**
Lemon icing (see below) as desired

1. Mix all ingredients in a bowl by hand. Add a little more water if necessary in case the dough is too hard to form a log shape.

2. Press into the muffin mold. As it does not rise, top up the mixture to make it look like a "muffin" shape.

3. Remove from the mold and place onto the mesh screen and dehydrate at 105-115° F/ 41-46° C for about 8 hours until dry outside but soft inside.

4. Serve with lemon icing on top or on the side.

# Lemon Icing

Yields 3/4 cup                                                    blender needed

½   cup (65g) cashew nuts, soaked

5   tablespoons coconut oil, melted if solid

2   tablespoons honey or liquid sweetener of your choice

2   tablespoons lemon juice

1   teaspoon lemon zest or a few drops lemon essential oil

⅛   teaspoon salt

1. Blend all ingredients until smooth and refrigerate for 1 hour to set.

# Carrot Muffins with Vanilla Frosting

This is a great way of recycling the carrot pulp after making carrot juice! Simple muffins go perfectly with rich, creamy frosting! What a luxury!

Yields 12 of 2 inch/5cm mini muffins
Mini silicon muffin mold (see FYI on page 37),
blender and dehydrator needed

4½    cups carrot pulp (the remains after making carrot juice)
1¼    cups (190g) ground almond (almond powder)  (see page 25 in the Techniques and Advance Preparation chapter for grinding)
2      tablespoons ground flaxseeds (see page 25 in the Techniques and Advance Preparation chapter for grinding)
3      tablespoons coconut oil, melted if solid
5      tablespoons date paste (see page 31 in the Techniques and Advance Preparation chapter)
4      tablespoons raisins, roughly chopped
4      tablespoons walnuts, roughly chopped
½      teaspoon vanilla extract
1      teaspoon cinnamon powder
¼      teaspoon nutmeg powder
        Pinch clove powder
        Pinch salt

## Garnish:
Vanilla frosting (see next page) as desired

1. Mix all ingredients in a bowl by hand and press into the muffin mold. As it does not rise, top up the mixture to make it look like a "muffin" shape.
2. Remove from the mold and place onto the mesh screen and dehydrate at 105-115° F/ 41-46° C for about 8 hours until dry outside but soft inside.
3. Garnish with vanilla frosting on top or on the side.


### Variation: Carrot Cake
If you want to make carrot cake, fill the dough into the cake pan, pour the frosting on top, and refrigerate until set! Much easier indeed, not even a dehydrator is needed!!

# Vanilla Frosting

Yields ¾ cup                                          blender needed

- ½     cup (65g) cashew nuts, soaked
- 6     tablespoons coconut oil
- 2     tablespoons honey or liquid sweetener of your choice
- 1     tablespoon lemon juice
- 2     teaspoons vanilla extract
      Pinch salt

1. Blend all ingredients until smooth and refrigerate for 1 hour to set.

**FYI:** Mini silicon muffin molds (see page 15 in the Tools For Raw Sweets chapter to see a photo) are very useful. They are easy to remove straight after you fill the dough in order to dehydrate so that they will have a perfect outcome, crunchy outside and soft inside.

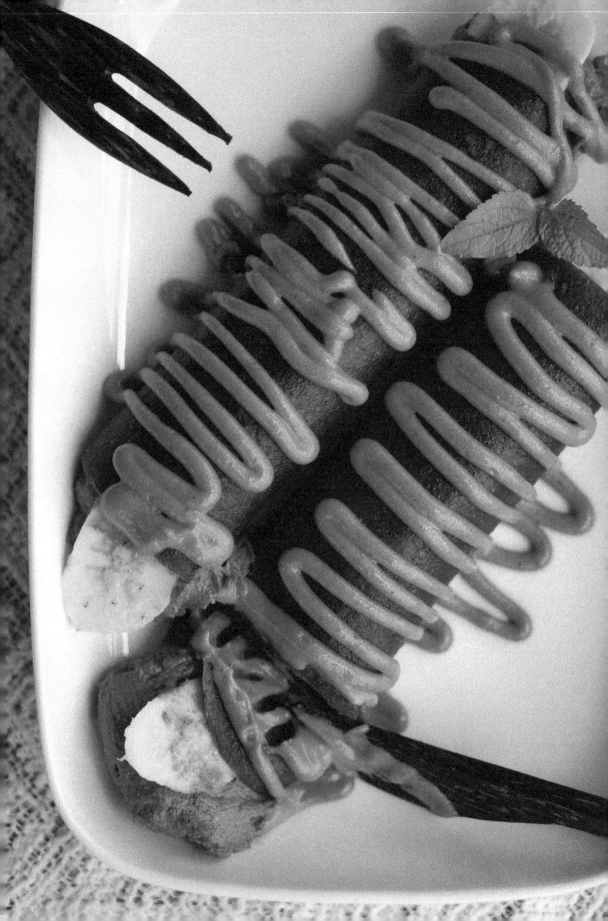

# Chocolate Crepes

Wow-hoo, this is really a delicacy, such a luxury breakfast! Makes the whole day special!

Yields 9 crepes                                                    blender and dehydrator needed

4½  cups chopped bananas

1½  cups water

3    tablespoons cacao powder

1½  tablespoons ground chia seeds (see page 25 Techniques and Advance Preparation chapter for grinding)

## Assembly:

4-5  bananas, sliced

1½  cups homemade Nutella (see page 49 in the Sweet Creams and Sauces chapter)

Maca caramel sauce (see page 53 in the Sweet Creams and Sauces chapter) as desired

1. Blend all ingredients except for ground chia seeds until smooth.
2. Add chia seeds and blend until evenly blended.
3. Spread 1/4 cup of the mixture onto nonstick sheets and form into a 6 inch/15 cm diameter circle with offset spatula.
4. Dehydrate at 105-115 ° F/ 41-46 ° C for about 4-6 hours or until dry on top, then flip it onto the mesh screen and continue to dehydrate for a few hours or until completely dry but still pliable.
5. To assemble, place 2½ tablespoons homemade Nutella and sliced banana on the crepe, roll over to the end, then decorate with maca caramel sauce on top.

# Strawberry Roll

Super simple to make, so trust me and try! It's rewarding to make it one night before :)

Yields 8 rolls                                          blender and dehydrator needed

## Strawberry wrapper:
5     cups strawberries; if unavailable, use any berries

3     tablespoons psyllium husk

## Assembly:
2-4  mangos, sliced

1½   cups Vanilla Whippy Cream (see page 51 in the Sweet Creams and Sauces chapter)

Chocolate Ganache Sauce (see page 53 in the Sweet Creams and Sauces chapter) as desired

1.  For the strawberry wrapper, blend strawberries until smooth, and then add psyllium husk and blend until evenly blended.
2.  Spread onto two of the nonstick sheets and dehydrate at 105-115 ° F/ 41-46 ° C for 8 hours or until completely dry but still pliable.
3.  Cut into 4 squares.
4.  To assemble, place 3 tablespoons vanilla whippy cream and sliced mango on the crepe, roll over to the end, then decorate with chocolate ganache sauce on top.

# Banana Bread with Coconut Cream Cheese

This nice and moist, slightly sweet banana bread is the most popular breakfast at yoga retreats!

Yields 6 inch/15cm lengthwise bread loaf          food processor and dehydrator needed

1½  cups chopped bananas

1    cup (120g) walnuts, soaked

2    tablespoons date paste (see page 31 Techniques and Advance Preparation chapter)

½    teaspoon cinnamon powder

     pinch nutmeg powder

     pinch salt

2    tablespoons water

1    cup any nut pulp (the remains after squeezing milk) (see page 24 Techniques and Advance Preparation chapter)

2    tablespoons ground flaxseeds (see page 25 Techniques and Advance Preparation chapter)

## Serving:
Coconut cream cheese (see page 50 in the Sweet Creams and Sauces chapter) as desired

1. Process all ingredients except for the nut pulp and flaxseeds until pureed in the food processor.
2. Transfer into a bowl and add nut pulp and flaxseed, mix until well combined.
3. Form into a 6 inch/15cm long log shape. Add a little more water if necessary in case the dough is too hard to form a log shape.
4. Place onto the nonstick sheet and dehydrate at 105-115° F/41-46° C for about 3 hours.
5. Remove from dehydrator and place onto a chopping board and slice into 0.7 inch/2cm thick pieces.
6. Place onto the mesh screen and continue to dehydrate at 105-115° F/41-46° C for about 8 hours until crunchy on the outside but soft on the inside.
7. Serve with coconut cream cheese.

# Pecan and Cranberry Sweetbread

Enjoy with all kinds of creams and sauces! The combination with fig compote and coconut cream cheese is a killer!

Yields 7 inch/18cm lengthwise bread loaf
dehydrator needed

2   cups any nut pulp (the remains after squeezing milk) (see page 24 in the Techniques and Advance Preparation chapter)

⅔   cup orange juice

½   cup pecan nuts, chopped

½   cup cranberries, chopped

6   tablespoons date paste (see page 31 in the Techniques and Advance Preparation chapter)

6   tablespoons ground flaxseeds (see page 25 in the Techniques and Advance Preparation chapter for grinding)

3   tablespoons coconut oil, melted if solid

¼   teaspoon salt

## Serving:

Fig compote and coconut cream cheese (see page 50 in the Sweet Creams and Sauces chapter) as desired

1.  Mix all ingredients in a bowl by hand.
2.  Form into a 7 inch/18cm long log shape. Add a little more orange juice or water if necessary in case the dough is too hard to form a log shape.
3.  Place onto the nonstick sheet and dehydrate at 105-115° F/41-46° C for about 3 hours.
4.  Remove from dehydrator and place onto a chopping board and slice into 0.4 inch/1cm thick pieces.
5.  Place onto the mesh screen and continue to dehydrate at 105-115 ° F/41-46 ° C for about 4-6 hours until crunchy on the outside but soft on the inside.
6.  Enjoy with fig compote and coconut cream cheese.

# Acai Bowl with Superfood Toppings

Best way to start the day! This powerful super-berry bowl is packed with protein, antioxidants, and keeps you feel amazing throughout your day! Top with your favorite superfoods to make it special!

Serves 2

¾ cup nut milk of your choice (see page 23 in the Techniques and Advance Preparation chapter)

1 frozen banana

2 cups frozen blueberries

1½ tablespoons acai powder

1 tablespoon sweetener of your choice if necessary (optional)

## Toppings:

Slices of banana, fresh blueberries or any fruits in season, superfood of your choice such as goji berries, cacao nibs, desiccated coconut, or buckwheat granola to taste

1. Blend all ingredients until smooth.
2. Garnish with your favorite toppings to serve.

# SWEET CREAMS AND SAUCES

Dreamy yummy creams and sauces without any dairy! It's a revolution!

# Fig Compote

Dried fruits soaked in orange juice with spices ⋯ this simple but blast of flavors will brighten up your morning!

Yields 3 cups

| | | | |
|---|---|---|---|
| 1 | cup orange juice | 1 | cup (150g) sliced dry figs |
| 2 | tablespoons raisins | 2 | tablespoons sliced dry apricot |
| 2 | tablespoons goji berries | 1 | tablespoon ginger juice |
| ½ | teaspoon nutmeg powder | 1 | stick cinnamon |

1. Soak all the ingredients in orange juice and keep in the fridge for more than 4 hours or overnight.

# Homemade Nutella

Hazelnuts and chocolate— no words needed—it's a winner! It is so great with bananas or any fruits and of course with crackers and crepes! You can keep it in the fridge for a week if you have enough discipline :) It never ever last in my kitchen.

Yields 1½ cups                                                                          blender needed

1    cup (140g) hazelnuts

¾    cup nut milk of your choice (see page 23 in the Techniques and Advance Preparation chapter)

4    tablespoons (55g) melted cacao butter

4    tablespoons yacon syrup (see FYI below) or molasses or maple syrup

2    tablespoons coconut oil, melted if solid

2    teaspoons vanilla extract

      pinch salt

4    tablespoons cacao powder

1. Blend all ingredients except for cacao powder until smooth.
2. Add cacao powder and blend until well combined.
3. Pour into a container and refrigerate for 1-2 hours or until set.

**FYI: Yacon Syrup**
Yacon is a tuber native in South America. It is rich in antioxidants and is low in glycemic index. Sold as dried powder or syrup, which has a dark brown, rich molasses-like flavor.

# Coconut Cream Cheese

Delicious, thick, tart cream cheese! I love to mix it with chopped raisins or dates and walnuts, then spread onto thin crackers! Sooooo delicious! Also it is good to mix with chopped herbs and olives for a savory version! Yumm!

Yields 1¼ cups                                                                 blender needed

1     cup (130g) cashew nuts, soaked
6     tablespoons lemon juice
6     tablespoons coconut oil, melted if solid
4     tablespoons maple syrup
½     teaspoon salt

1. Blend all ingredients until smooth.
2. Pour into a container and refrigerate for 1-2 hours or until set.

# Blueberry Jam

There's nothing like homemade jam! Uncooked, raw jam is actually super easy! 1 minute and it is done! You can try with any other fruits! Enjoy!

Yields 2½ cups                                                        food processor needed

3     cups blueberries
½     cup date paste (see page 31 in the Techniques and Advance Preparation chapter)
1     teaspoon lemon juice

1. Set aside 2 cups blueberries and process all the rest of the ingredients in a food processor.
2. Add 2 cups blueberries and blend for a few seconds.

> **FYI:** In case it is too watery, especially when you are using frozen berries, try adding a little bit of psyllium husk at the end and blend. It will suck up the liquid after some time. Be careful not to add too much, though!

# Vanilla Whippy Cream (photo on the next page)

Heaven! My favorite thing in the world!

Yields 2 cups                                                          blender needed

½   cup (65g) cashew nuts, soaked

¾   cup nut milk of your choice (see page 24 of Techniques and Advance Preparation chapter)

4-5  tablespoons honey or liquid sweetener of your choice

4    tablespoons coconut oil, melted if solid

1    tablespoon lecithin                    1    teaspoon lemon juice

1    teaspoon vanilla extract                   Pinch salt

½   cup vanilla beans, scraped to use only seeds (optional)

6    tablespoons Irish moss paste (see page 30 of Techniques and Advance Preparation chapter)

1.  Blend all ingredients except for Irish moss paste until smooth.
2.  Add Irish moss paste and blend until well incorporated.
3.  Pour into a container and refrigerate for a couple of hours or until set.

### Variations:
**Strawberry Whippy Cream:** Replace nut milk with 1¼ cups strawberries.
**Chocolate Whippy Cream:** Add 2 tablespoons cacao powder and 1 more tablespoon honey.
**Green Tea Whippy Cream:** Add 2 teaspoons green tea and 1 more tablespoon honey.
**Cinnamon Whippy Cream:** Add 1 teaspoon cinnamon powder.

# Avocado Whippy Cream (photo on the next page)

Avocado for sweet cream? Yes! It's perfect for dessert indeed as of its smooth, thick consistency without adding much flavor. Whip up your imagination with this yummy zesty green-y cream.

Yields 2 cups                                                          blender needed

2 cups chopped avocado (about 2 avocados)

4 tablespoons honey or liquid sweetener of your choice

1 tablespoon lemon juice

1 teaspoon vanilla extract

1.  Blend all ingredients until smooth. Add a little coconut oil if necessary to facilitate easy blending.

# Maca Caramel Cream Sauce

Earthy maca goes so well with this nice and rich caramel flavor!

Yields ¾ cup                                                                blender needed

½   cup (60g) macadamia nuts, soaked

3   tablespoons yacon syrup or molasses or maple syrup (for yacon, see FYI on page 49 of Homemade Nutella recipe in this chapter)

3   tablespoons coconut oil, melted if solid

1   tablespoon maca powder

2   teaspoons vanilla extract

¼   teaspoon salt

2   tablespoons water

1. Blend all ingredients until smooth.


# Chocolate Ganache Sauce

Watch out! It's so delicious you'll want to pour it onto everything!

Yields ½ cup                                                                blender needed

7   tablespoons cacao powder

4   tablespoons honey or liquid sweetener of your choice

4   tablespoons coconut oil, melted if solid

½   teaspoon salt

2   tablespoons water

1. Blend all ingredients until smooth.

# PUDDINGS AND MOUSSES

I love creamy, silky, heavenly puddings! They are wonderful as an easily digestible breakfast, as well as baby food for a busy mom!

# Chocolate Banana Chia Pudding

This tiny little seed is packed with easily digestible protein, vitamins and minerals, and essential fatty acids. Morning chia keeps you going all day!

Serves 2

2    cups nut milk of your choice (see page 23 in the Techniques and Advance Preparation chapter)

4    tablespoons chia seeds

3    tablespoons cacao powder

1    tablespoon honey or liquid sweetener of your choice

1    teaspoon vanilla extract

Pinch salt

A few deseeded dates, chopped

1    banana, chopped

**FYI:** If you want to have it ready sooner, use slightly warm nut milk, and it will be ready in about 30 minutes, as chia seeds absorb the warm liquid quickly.

1. Mix all ingredients except for chia seeds, dates, and banana in the bowl.
2. Add chia seeds and mix with whisk for a few minutes.
3. Fold in dates and refrigerate overnight (see FYI above).
4. Add chopped banana before serving.

# Chai and Goji Chia Porridge

When I was in India, I was obsessed with anything chai flavor. Thick, sweet coconut milk with Indian chai spices is the killer!

Serves 2

3    cups coconut milk or any nut milk of your choice (see page 23 in the Techniques and Advance Preparation chapter)

6    tablespoons chia seeds

2    tablespoons honey or liquid sweetener of your choice

1    teaspoon vanilla extract

¼    teaspoon cardamom powder

4    tablespoons goji berries or raisins

½    teaspoon cinnamon powder

Pinch salt

1. Mix all the ingredients except for chia seeds in the bowl.
2. Add chia seeds and mix with whisk for a few minutes.
3. Refrigerate overnight (see FYI at right).

**FYI:** If you want to have it ready sooner, use slightly warm nut milk, and it will be ready in about 30 minutes, as chia seeds absorb the warm liquid quickly.

# Dragon Coconut Pudding

Pretty pink-colored dragon fruit makes it special!

Serves 4~6                                                                 blender needed

2     cups coconut milk or any nut milk of your choice (see page 23 Techniques and Advance Preparation chapter)

1      cup soaked Irish moss (see page 30 in the Techniques and Advance Preparation chapter)

1     cup (130g) cashew nuts, soaked

⅓    cup honey or liquid sweetener of your choice

4     tablespoons coconut oil, melted if solid

1     tablespoon lecithin; if unavailable, it is ok to omit

1     teaspoon vanilla extract

¼    teaspoon cardamom powder

## Garnish:

1      dragon fruit, sliced; if unavailable, use any fruit of your choice

1. Blend 1 cup coconut milk and soaked Irish moss until slightly warm and Irish moss is completely dissolved.
2. Add all the rest of the ingredients and blend until smooth.
3. Pour into glasses and refrigerate for a few hours to set.
4. Garnish with dragon fruit to serve.

# Hazelnut Chocolate Mousse

So light and elegant ⋯ absolutely divine!

Serves 4-6                                                      blender needed

3     cups hazelnut milk (see page 23 in the Techniques and Advance Preparation chapter)
1     cup soaked Irish moss (see page 30 in the Techniques and Advance Preparation chapter)
¾-1 cup date paste (see page 31 in the Techniques and Advance Preparation chapter)
½     cup cacao powder                           1     teaspoon vanilla extract
4     tablespoons coconut oil, melted if solid   Pinch salt
1     tablespoon lecithin; if unavailable, it is ok to omit

## Garnish:
4-6  cacao beans

1. Blend 1 cup of hazelnut milk and soaked Irish moss until slight warm and Irish moss is completely dissolved.
2. Add all the rest of the ingredients and blend until smooth.
3. Pour into glasses and refrigerate for a few hours to set.
4. Garnish with cacao beans to serve.

# Strawberry Mousse

Reminds me of my sweet childhood, yummy mummy strawberry sweet dream …

Serves 4~6                                                      blender needed

1     cup nut milk of your choice (see page 23 in the Techniques and Advance Preparation chapter)
1     cup soaked Irish moss (see page 30 the Techniques and Advance Preparation chapter)
2½   cups strawberries                           ½     cup (65g) cashew nuts, soaked
⅓    cup honey or liquid sweetener of your choice
4     tablespoons coconut oil, melted if solid
1     tablespoon lecithin; if unavailable, it is ok to omit
2     teaspoons lemon juice                       1     teaspoon vanilla extract

## Garnish:
½    cup strawberries, sliced

1. Blend nut milk and soaked Irish moss until slight warm and Irish moss is completely dissolved.
2. Add all the rest of the ingredients and blend until smooth.
3. Pour into glasses and refrigerate for a few hours to set.
4. Garnish with sliced strawberries to serve.

# White Chocolate Mousse with Blueberry Sauce

Creamy, whippy white chocolate comes with gorgeous berry sauce . . . scrumptious!

Serves 4–6                                                                              blender needed

2½  cups nut milk of your choice (see page 23 in the Techniques and Advance Preparation chapter)

1    cup soaked Irish moss (see page 30 in the Techniques and Advance Preparation chapter)

½    cup (65g) cashew nuts, soaked

⅓    cup honey or liquid sweetener of your choice

4    tablespoons (55g) melted cacao butter

1    tablespoon lecithin; if unavailable, it is ok to omit

2    teaspoons vanilla extract

## Garnish:

Blueberry jam (see page 50 in the Sweet Creams and Sauces chapter) as desired

1. Blend 1 cup of nut milk and soaked Irish moss until slight warm and Irish moss is completely dissolved.
2. Add all the rest of the ingredients and blend until smooth.
3. Pour into glasses and refrigerate for a few hours to set.
4. Garnish with blueberry jam to serve.

# CAKES, DOUGHNUTS, AND CRUMBLES

When you are bored with wobbly, creamy texture, then it's time for a change! Try cakes for a bit of an elaborated dessert! Indeed, by that time, you have nut pulps packed in your freezer waiting to be used :) By the way, in case there is leftover from the cake dough, you can make into cookie shapes and dehydrate them! The leftovers turn into cookies! It's my secret stash when I cater for a retreat :)

# Tiramisu

Café Gratitude cookbooks are my favorite books, especially *Sweet Gratitude*! I often dream of cakes and cookies while doing yoga in the morning :) and cannot wait to try the new recipes. (Don't tell my yoga teacher!) This recipe is inspired by *"Sweet Gratitude"*.

Yields 9 pieces
Blender and 8.3x8.3 inch/21x21cm loose-bottom square cake pan needed

## Coffee cake:

2½   cups nut flour (dried, powdered nut pulp, (see page 24 in the Techniques and Advance Preparation chapter) (also see FYI below)

1    cup + 2 tablespoons (300ml) date paste (see page 31 in the Techniques and Advance Preparation chapter)

6    tablespoons cacao powder

6    tablespoons coconut oil, melted if solid

4    tablespoons water or cold press coffee

2-3  teaspoons coffee extract or 15 drops medicine flower's coffee extract (see page 18 in the Staple Ingredients and Raw Alternatives chapter) (also see FYI below)

¼    teaspoon salt

## Chocolate mousse:

¾    cup nut milk of your choice (see page 23 in the Techniques and Advance Preparation chapter)

½    cup (65g) cashew nuts, soaked

½    cup + 1 tablespoon (140ml) date paste (see page 31 in the Techniques and Advance Preparation chapter)

1    tablespoon lecithin; if unavailable, it is ok to omit

½    teaspoon vanilla extract

⅛    teaspoon salt

7    tablespoon Irish moss paste (100ml) (see page 30 in the Techniques and Advance Preparation chapter)

3    tablespoons cacao powder

2    tablespoons coconut oil, melted if solid


**FYI:** If using pulp instead of nut flour, just reduce water quantity.


**FYI:** If natural coffee extract is unavailable, replace with 1 double shot espresso.

## Vanilla cream:

1½ cups nut milk of your choice (see page 23 in the Techniques and Advance Preparation chapter)

1 cup (130g) cashew nuts, soaked

4 tablespoons honey or liquid sweetener of your choice

2 tablespoons lecithin

1 teaspoon vanilla extract

    pinch salt

7 tablespoons Irish moss paste (100ml) (see page 30 in the Techniques and Advance Preparation chapter)

¼ cup coconut oil, melted if solid

## Garnish:

    Cacao powder as required

9 pieces cacao beans

1. For the coffee cake, mix all ingredients in a bowl. The consistency should be easily to hold together by hand. If it is too dry, add a little liquid to adjust the consistency.
2. Press into the lightly greased container, then place in the freezer while making the chocolate mousse.
3. For the chocolate mousse, blend all ingredients except for Irish moss paste, cacao powder, and coconut oil until smooth.
4. Add Irish moss paste, cacao powder, and coconut oil, then blend until well incorporated.
5. Pour onto the coffee cake, flatten, and place in the freezer while making the vanilla cream. (If more than 30 minutes, move to the fridge.)
6. For the vanilla cream, blend all ingredients except for Irish moss paste and coconut oil until smooth.
7. Add Irish moss paste and coconut oil and blend until well incorporated.
8. Take the chocolate mousse out of freezer and make sure it is set. If not, place back in the freezer until it sets.
9. Pour the vanilla cream gently on top of the chocolate mousse and refrigerate for a couple of hours or overnight until set.
10. To garnish, cut into 9 pieces or the desirable size, sift the cacao powder on top and decorate with cacao beans in the center of each cake.

# Green Tea Tiramisu  (photo on the next page)

Tiramisu a la Japan! Rum raisins and green tea are the best matching flavors!

Yields 9 pieces
Blender and 8.3x8.3 inch/21x21cm loose-bottom square cake pan needed

## Almond cake:
1¼   cups nut flour (dried, powdered nut pulp, <u>see page 24</u> in the Techniques and Advance Preparation chapter) (also <u>see FYI below</u>)

1½   cups (225g) ground almond (<u>see page 25</u> in the Techniques and Advance Preparation chapter for grinding)

½    cup date paste (<u>see page 31</u> in the Techniques and Advance Preparation chapter)

4    tablespoons coconut oil, melted if solid

¼    teaspoon almond extract or 1 teaspoon vanilla extract

⅛    teaspoon salt

4-6  tablespoons water (quantity may vary depending on the variety of nut flour)

## Green tea mousse:
¾    cup nut milk of your choice (<u>see page 23</u> in the Techniques and Advance Preparation chapter)

½    cup (65g) cashew nuts, soaked

½    cup coconut sugar syrup or liquid sweetener of your choice

1    tablespoon lecithin; if unavailable, it is ok to omit

1    teaspoon vanilla extract

     pinch salt

7    tablespoons (100ml)  Irish moss paste (<u>see page 30</u> in the Techniques and Advance Preparation chapter)

1½   tablespoons green tea powder

2    tablespoons coconut oil, melted if solid


FYI: If using pulp instead of nut flour, just reduce water quantity.

## Rum raisin cream:

1½ cups nut milk of your choice (see page 23 in the Techniques and Advance Preparation chapter)

1 cup (130g) cashew nuts, soaked

4 tablespoons honey or liquid sweetener of your choice

2 tablespoons lecithin

1 teaspoon vanilla extract

1 teaspoon rum or 2-3 drops medicine flower's rum extract (see page 18 the Staple Ingredients and Raw Alternatives chapter)

pinch salt

7 tablespoons (100ml) Irish moss paste (see page 30 in the Techniques and Advance Preparation chapter)

¼ cup coconut oil, melted if solid

3 tablespoons raisins

## Garnish:

Green tea powder as required

1. For the almond cake, mix all ingredients in a bowl. The consistency should be easily to hold together by hand. If it is too dry, add a little liquid to adjust the consistency.

2. Press into the lightly greased container, then place in the freezer while making the green tea mousse.

3. For the green tea mousse, blend all ingredients except for Irish moss paste, green tea powder, and coconut oil until smooth.

4. Add Irish moss paste, green tea powder, and coconut oil, then blend until well incorporated.

5. Pour onto the almond cake, flatten, and place in the freezer while making the rum raisin cream. (If more than 30 minutes, move to the fridge.)

6. For the rum raisin cream, blend all ingredients except for Irish moss paste, coconut oil and raisins until smooth.

7. Add Irish moss paste and coconut oil and blend until well incorporated.

8. Add raisins and blend for a few seconds.

9. Take the green tea mousse out of freezer and make sure it is set. If not, place back in the freezer until it sets.

10. Pour the rum raisin cream gently on top of green tea mousse and refrigerate for a couple of hours or overnight until set.

11. To garnish, cut into 9 pieces or the desirable size, and sift the green tea powder on top.

### Variation: Green Tea Ice Cream Tiramisu

Use green tea ice cream (see page 157 for the variation of Rum Raisin Ice Cream in the Ice Cream chapter) instead of green tea mousse layer, and use Rum Raisin Ice Cream (see page 152 of the Ice Cream chapter) instead of the rum raisin cream layer!

# Strawberry Shortcake

My childhood favorite birthday cake in raw!

Yields 8-9 inch/21-23cm size cake
Blender and 8-9 inch/21-23cm bottom-removal cake mold needed

## Vanilla cake:

3¼ cups nut flour (dried, powdered nut pulp, see page 24 in the Techniques and Advance Preparation chapter) (see FYI below)

2 cups (300g) ground almonds (see page 25 in the Techniques and Advance Preparation chapter for grinding)

1 cup date paste (see page 31 in the Techniques and Advance Preparation chapter)

½ cup (140ml) coconut oil, melted if solid

1 teaspoon vanilla extract

¼ teaspoon salt

4-8 tablespoons water (quantity may vary, depending on the variety of nut flour)

## Coconut cream:

1½ cups coconut milk (see page 23 in the Techniques and Advance Preparation chapter); if unavailable, use any nut milk

1 cup soaked Irish moss (see page 30 in the Techniques and Advance Preparation chapter)

1 cup (130g) cashew nuts, soaked

6 tablespoons honey or liquid sweetener of your choice

2 teaspoons lemon juice

½ vanilla beans, scraped to use only the seeds (optional)

2 teaspoons vanilla extract

 Pinch salt

6 tablespoons coconut oil, melted if solid

2 tablespoons lecithin

## Assembly:

2 cups strawberries

FYI: If using pulp instead of nut
flour, just reduce water quantity.

1. For the vanilla cake, place all ingredients in a bowl and mix by hand until well incorporated. The consistency should be easily to hold together by hand. If it is too dry, add a little liquid to adjust the consistency.
2. Press half the dough into the lightly greased pan, and place in the freezer while making the coconut cream.
3. For the coconut cream, blend 1 cup of coconut milk and soaked Irish moss until slightly warm and Irish moss is completely dissolved, then set aside.
4. Blend all the rest of the ingredients for the coconut cream in a blender until smooth, add Irish moss mixture, and blend again until well blended.
5. Divide the cream into halves and keep half in the fridge for 2-3 hours to set.
6. Pour the half of "the remaining half" cream onto the vanilla cake, lay down 2 cups of sliced strawberries over the cream, cover with the rest of the cream, and place in the freezer for 1 hour or until completely set.
7. When the cream is completely set, gently place the rest of vanilla cake dough and press firmly.
8. Take out the cream kept in the fridge and mix by a whisk to make it smooth.
9. Spread 1/2 cup of cream on top of the cake evenly.
10. The rest of the cream is for decoration. If the cream is too soft for piping, refrigerate for another hour or until completely set.
11. Transfer the well-set cream into a piping bag with a star (or any shape) nozzle, pipe on top to decorate, and garnish with the rest of strawberries.
12. Refrigerate for another a couple hours or overnight to set.

### Variation: Chocolate Strawberry Shortcake

Reduce the amount of ground almonds to 1¾ cups and add 4 tablespoons cacao powder.

# Lemon Poppy Seed Cake (photo on the next page)

Classic! This is great to make into cupcakes as well!

Yields 8-9 inch /21-23cm size cake
Blender and 8-9 inch/21-23cm bottom-removal cake mold needed

## Poppy-seed cake:

3½ cups nut flour (dried, powdered nut pulp, see page 24 in the Techniques and Advance Preparation chapter)(see FYI below)

1 cup (150g) ground almonds (see page 25 in the Techniques and Advance Preparation chapter for grinding)

1 cup + 2 tablespoons date paste (see page 31 in the Techniques and Advance Preparation chapter)

¾ cup coconut oil, melted if solid

6 tablespoons lemon juice

2 tablespoons poppy seeds

1 teaspoon vanilla extract

¼ teaspoon salt

2 tablespoons lemon zest or a few drops lemon essential oil

2-4 tablespoons water (quantity may vary depending on the variety of nut flour)

## Lemon cream:

1½ cups nut milk of your choice (see page 23 in the Techniques and Advance Preparation chapter)

1 cup soaked Irish moss (see page 30 in the Techniques and Advance Preparation chapter)

1 cup (130g) cashew nuts, soaked

½ cup honey or liquid sweetener of your choice

3 tablespoons lemon juice

1 teaspoon pumpkin powder or 1/4 teaspoon turmeric powder (optional for yellow color)

2 teaspoons vanilla extract

⅛ teaspoon salt

2 tablespoons lecithin

½ cup coconut oil, melted if solid

## Garnish:

1-3 teaspoons poppy seeds

Slices of lemon, tossed with maple syrup and dehydrated overnight (optional) as needed; if unavailable, use slices of fresh lemon

1. For the poppy-seed cake, place all ingredients in a bowl and mix by hand until well incorporated. The consistency should be easily to hold together by hand. If it is too dry, add a little liquid to adjust the consistency.
2. Press half the dough into the lightly greased pan, and place in the freezer while making the lemon cream.
3. For the lemon cream, blend 1 cup nut milk and soaked Irish moss until slightly warm and Irish moss is completely dissolved, then set aside.
4. Blend all the rest of the ingredients for the lemon cream in a blender until smooth, add Irish moss mixture, and blend again until well blended.
5. Divide into halves and keep half in the fridge for 2-3 hours to set.
6. Pour the rest half cream onto the poppy-seed cake and place in the freezer for 1 hour or until completely set.
7. When the cream is set, gently place the remaining half of the poppy-seed cake dough and press firmly.
8. Take out the cream kept in the fridge and mix with a whisk to make it smooth.
9. Spread ½ cup of cream on top of the cake evenly.
10. The rest of the cream is for decoration. If the cream is too soft for piping, refrigerate for another hour or until completely set.
11. Transfer the set cream into a piping bag with a round nozzle and pipe on top to decorate.
12. Refrigerate for another a couple hours or overnight to set.
13. Garnish with a sprinkle of poppy seeds and dehydrated lemon if desired.

FYI: If using pulp instead of nut flour, just reduce water quantity.

# Fruit Cake

Abundant fruits, spices, and moistness make this a nice and rich luxury. Enjoy with vanilla whippy cream!

Yields 15 of 2 inch/5cm mini cakes
Mini silicon muffin mold (see FYI on page 36 on carrot muffins recipe in the Breakfast for a Sweet Tooth chapter) and dehydrator (optional) needed

## Cake dough:
1   cup (150g) ground  almonds (see page 25 in the Techniques and Advance Preparation chapter for grinding)
1   cup nut flour (dried, powdered nut pulp, see page 24 in the Techniques and Advance Preparation chapter) (see FYI below)
4   tablespoons coconut oil, melted if solid
2   tablespoons date paste (see page 31 in the Techniques and Advance Preparation chapter)
¼   teaspoon salt

## Marinated dried fruits:
1   cup (150g) raisins
½   cup (75g) sliced dried apricot
1   stick cinnamon
½   split vanilla beans or 2 teaspoons vanilla extract
1   teaspoon rum or 2-3 drops medicine flower's rum extract (see page 18 in the Staple Ingredients and Raw Alternatives chapter)

½   cup (75g) sliced dried fig
¾   cup orange juice
    pinch salt

## Garnish:
1-2  cups vanilla whippy cream (see page 51 in the Sweet Creams and Sauces chapter)

1. For the marinated dried fruits, mix all ingredients in a bowl and marinate overnight in the fridge.
2. For the cake dough, mix all ingredients by hand until well incorporated.
3. Take vanilla beans and cinnamon stick out of marinated dried fruits.
4. Fold in the marinated dried fruits into cake dough mixture.
5. Press into the mini silicon muffin mold.
6. Refrigerate for a couple of hours to set.
7. Take out from the mold then dehydrate at 135° F/57° C for a few hours or until dry on the outside but soft on the inside. (Optional) (If longer than that, bring it down to 105-115° F/41-46° C)
8. Serve with vanilla whippy cream.

FYI: If using pulp instead of nut flour, reduce coconut oil to 3 tablespoons

# Chocolate Brownies with Ice Cream and Ganache

Holy moly, this delicious dessert is for everyone for any occasion!

Yields 8x6 inch/20x15cm size brownie / serves 12
Food processor and 8x6 inch/20x15cm size container needed

## Brownies:

2¼  cups (270g) walnuts

⅓  cup cacao powder

½  teaspoon cherry extract or 2-3 drops medicine flower's cherry extract (see page 18 in the Staple Ingredients and Raw Alternatives chapter)

¼  teaspoon salt

¾-1 cup (130g ~170g) deseeded dates, chopped

¼  cup cacao nibs

⅓  cup (50g) chopped raisins

## Garnish:

2- 2½   cups vanilla ice cream (see page 153 in the Ice Cream chapter)

Chocolate ganache sauce (see page 53 in the Sweet Creams and Sauces chapter) as desired

1.  Process 2 cups walnuts, cacao powder, cherry extract, and salt in the food processor into powder.
2.  Add dates while processing until evenly combined.
3.  Add 1/4 cup walnuts, cacao nibs, and raisins and process until just enough incorporated.
4.  Press into the lightly greased container and refrigerate for 1-2 hours to set.
5.  Cut into 12 pieces or the desired size and serve with the scoop of vanilla ice cream and chocolate ganache on top.

# Samoan Coconut Dream Cake

This is award-winning cake in my entire dessert world that I know :) What's on earth Samoan cake? It means our-all-time-favorite triple combination of coconut + chocolate + caramel! Yes, we LOVE them all, aren't we :) Thanks to fragrant vanilla cake, my favorite chef, for the inspiration.

Yields 8-9 inch/21-23cm size cake
Blender, food processor and 8-9 inch/21-23cm bottom-removal cake mold needed

## Crust:
1    cup nut flour (see page 24 in the Techniques and Advance Preparation chapter)

½    cup (70g) almonds        1 ½   tablespoons cacao nibs

2    tablespoons coconut oil, melted of solid     ¼    teaspoon salt

3    tablespoons coconut sugar syrup or liquid sweetener of your choice

## Coconut cream filling:
2 ¼   cups (290g) cashew nuts, soaked

½    cup water

½    cup honey or liquid sweetener of your choice

½    cup coconut oil, melted of solid

4    tablespoons (55g) melted cacao butter

4    tablespoons (60g) coconut butter (see FYI below)

1    teaspoon vanilla extract

¼    teaspoon salt

## Chocolate layer:
4    tablespoons cacao powder

1    tablespoon maple syrup or liquid sweetener of your choice

1    tablespoon water

## Caramel cream:
1    cup dates paste (see page 31 in the Techniques and Advance Preparation chapter)

½    cup (120g) coconut butter (see FYI below)     ¼    teaspoon salt

4    tablespoons coconut oil, melted of solid     2    tablespoons maple syrup

6-7   drops medicine flower's caramel extract (optional) (see page 18 in the Staple Ingredients and Raw Alternatives chapter)

FYI: Coconut butter is different from coconut oil. If it is not available, you can make it at home from shredded dry coconut. (See page 28 for Homemade Nut Butter in Techniques and Advance Preparation chapter for grinding)

**Garnish:**

Chocolate ganashe sauce (<u>see page 53</u> in the Sweet Creams and Sauces chapter) as required

1. For the crust, in the food processor, process almond first into powder, then add nut flour, cacao nibs and salt to process into powder, and then add maple syrup and coconut oil while processing. The consistency should be easily to hold together by hand. If it is too dry, add a little liquid ingredient to adjust the consistency.
2. Press the mixture into a lightly greased pan and set aside in the fridge.
3. For the coconut cream filling, blend all ingredients until smooth.
4. Pour half of the filling onto the crust and place in the freezer to set for 30 minutes.
5. Add chocolate layer ingredients into the remaining mixture in the blender, blend until smooth, then pour on top of the coconut cream filling and place in the freezer to set for 30 minutes ~ 1hour.
6. For the caramel cream, blend all ingredients until smooth.
7. Take the cake out of freezer and make sure it is set. If not, place back in the freezer until it sets for another 30 minutes -1 hour. (While waiting for the cake to set, do not refrigerate the caramel cream to avoid hardening.)
8. Spread the caramel cream gently on top, flatten the surface, and then refrigerate for 4-6 hours or until set.
9. To garnish, take the cake out of the pan, and drizzle the chocolate ganashe sauce on top.

# Banana Carob Cake

This can be a nice and light breakfast or snack!

Yields 7x4 inch/18x10cm size cake
7x4 inch/18x10cm silicon pound cake mold and food
processor needed

1½  cups (225g) ground hazelnuts (see page 25
     in the Techniques and Advance Preparation
     chapter for grinding)

1½  cups nut pulp (see page 24 in the
     Techniques and Advance Preparation
     chapter)

5    tablespoons (50g) deseeded dates,
     finely chopped

4    tablespoons carob powder (see FYI
     below) if unavailable, use cacao powder

1    teaspoon vanilla extract

¼    teaspoon salt

4    tablespoons coconut oil, melted if solid

2    cups small chopped bananas

## Serving:
Slices of banana, Vanilla Whippy Cream (see page 51 in the Sweet Creams and Sauces chapter) and Maca Caramel Cream sauce (see page 53 in the Sweet Creams and Sauces chapter) as desired

1. Process all the ingredients except for coconut oil and banana in the food processor until the dates are well blended.
2. Add coconut oil and blend until well blended.
3. Transfer into a bowl and fold in the bananas.
4. Lightly grease the pound cake mold then line with parchment paper or plastic wrap.
5. Transfer into the mold and refrigerate for a couple of hours or until set.
6. When serving, turn it over and remove from the mold, slice into 1 inch/2cm thick pieces, serve with banana slices and vanilla whippy cream, and drizzle maca caramel cream sauce on top.

FYI: The carob tree is native to the Mediterranean region. Carob powder, the ground dry pod, is a nutritious, subtle sweet flavored powder, which is often used as cacao substitute since it doesn't contains caffeine.

# Caramel Doughnuts

What goes better with doughnuts than salted caramel? This is sure to be a hit. I'm just totally in love with these super cute little babies :)

Yields 12 doughnuts                                    blender and dehydrator needed

## Doughnuts:

1½   cups nut flour (dried, powdered nut pulp, see page 24 in the Techniques and Advance Preparation chapter) (see FYI below)

1½   cups (225g) ground almonds (see page 25 in the Techniques and Advance Preparation chapter for grinding)

½    cup maple syrup

4    tablespoons ground flaxseeds (see page 25 in the Techniques and Advance Preparation chapter for grinding)

3    tablespoons coconut oil, melted if solid

2    teaspoons vanilla extract

¼    teaspoon salt

½-¾  cup water (quantity may vary depending on the variety of nut flour)

## Salted Caramel frosting:

(need only half quantity for this recipe, yet this is a easy-to-make quantity)

1½   cups (180g) macadamia nuts, soaked           4   tablespoons maple syrup

6    tablespoons nut milk of your choice or water   1   tablespoon lucuma powder

6    tablespoons coconut oil, melted if solid

4-6  drops medicine flower's caramel extract (optional) (see page 18 in the Staple Ingredients and Raw Alternatives chapter)

2    teaspoons vanilla extract                        ½   teaspoon salt

## Garnish:

   Cacao nibs or chopped nuts as desired.

1. For the doughnuts, mix all ingredients in a bowl until well incorporated.

2. Divide the mixture into 12, form ball shapes, make a hole in the center with your finger, then place onto the mesh screen. If it cracks when forming the shape, add some more water to adjust the consistency.

3. Dehydrate at 105-115° F/41-46° C for about 8 hours or until dry on the outside but soft on the inside.

4. For the salted caramel frosting, blend all ingredients until smooth, refrigerate for 1 hour or until set, and then transfer into a small-nozzle squeeze bottle.

5. Pipe the caramel sauce onto the doughnuts and garnish with some cacao nibs or chopped nuts.

   **FYI:** If using pulp instead of nut flour, just reduce water quantity.

## Frosting Variation: Pink Lavender Frosting

Inspired by "fragrant vanilla cake," it makes super pretty looking doughnuts!

Yields 2 cups (need only half quantity for this recipe, yet this is a easy-to-make quantity)

1½  cups (200g) cashew nuts, soaked

1½  tablespoons beet juice; if unavailable, use 1 tablespoon strawberry powder

1   tablespoon water

4   tablespoons coconut oil, melted if solid

4   tablespoons honey or liquid sweetener of your choice

2   teaspoons lemon juice

2   teaspoons dry lavender flower

1   teaspoon vanilla extract

¼   teaspoon salt


1. Blend all ingredients until smooth.

# Peach Crumble with Vanilla Ice Cream

One of the simplest desserts, yet looks and taste gorgeous and never goes wrong. Enjoy the juiciness of ripe peaches in season! Try with other fruits such as cherries and any berries!

Yields 7x8 inch/18x24cm size crumble / serves 10-12
Food processor, dehydrator (optional) and a 7x8 inch/18x24cm size container needed

## Filling:
6 cups sliced peaches; if unavailable, use plums, pears, apples and berries

1 tablespoon honey or liquid sweetener of your choice

1 tablespoon lemon juice

½ teaspoon cardamom powder

## Crumble:
3 cups (360g) walnuts or pecan nuts

1 tablespoon coconut oil, melted if solid

¼ teaspoon nutmeg powder

½ cup (85g) deseeded dates, chopped

2 tablespoons maple syrup

1 teaspoon cinnamon powder

¼ teaspoon salt

## Serving:
Vanilla ice cream (see page 153 in Ice Cream chapter) as desired (optional)

1. For the filling, pulse 3 cups of peaches with the rest of the ingredients in the food processor lightly, transfer into a bowl, and mix with the rest of the peaches.
2. For the crumble, pulse walnuts into small chunks in the food processor.
3. Add all the rest of the ingredients and process until the mixture can hold together but is still crumbly. Do not overprocess into a paste.
4. To assemble, spread half the amount of the crumble onto a lightly greased container.
5. Place the filling onto it and cover with the rest of the crumble.
6. Warm in the dehydrator at 135° F/57° C for a few hours. (optional) (If longer than that, bring it down to 105-115° F/41-46° C)
7. Serve with vanilla ice cream. (optional)

# CHEESECAKE

Cheesecake is actually the easiest to make!
Change the fruits in the filling and explore
your own new recipes!

# Blueberry Cheesecake

Easy, never-fail dessert that makes everyone happy and smile!

Yields 8-9 inch/21-23cm cake

Blender, food processor, and 8-9 inch/21-23cm loose-bottom cake pan needed

## Crust:

1½  cups any nuts of your choice

2  tablespoons cacao powder

¼  teaspoon salt

¾  cup 130g) deseeded dates, chopped (adjust the quantity depending on the softness of dates)

## Blueberry cheesecake filling:

2¾  cups (350g) cashew nuts, soaked

2  cups blueberries

½  cup honey or liquid sweetener of your choice

4  tablespoons lemon juice

1  tablespoon lemon zest or a few drops lemon essential oil

1  teaspoon vanilla extract

¼  teaspoon salt

2  tablespoons lecithin; if unavailable, it is ok to omit

¾  cup (230ml) coconut oil, melted if solid, (for the lighter version, use ½ cup (140ml) coconut oil + ½ cup (120ml) Irish moss paste)

## Garnish:

Blueberries as desired (optional)

1. For the crust, process all the ingredients except for the dates in the food processor until well ground.
2. Add dates, little by little, while processing. The consistency should be enough to be held together by hand, but still easy to break. If it is too dry, add some more dates or coconut oil.
3. Press the mixture into a lightly greased pan and set aside in the fridge.
4. For the filling, blend all ingredients except for coconut oil (and Irish moss), until smooth.
5. Add coconut oil (and Irish moss) and blend evenly.
6. Pour onto the crust, garnish with some blueberries on top if desired and refrigerate for 8 hours or overnight until set.

# Mango Chocolate Cheesecake

This golden cheesecake is the most wanted golden combination of sweet, flavorful mango and rich chocolate! Delicious!

Yields 8-9 inch/21-23cm cake
Blender, food processor, and 8-9 inch/21-23cm loose-bottom cake pan needed

## Chocolate crust:

1¼   cups (190g) almonds

½     cup (38g) desiccated shredded coconut

2     tablespoons cacao powder          ¼   teaspoons salt

¾     cup (130g) deseeded dates, chopped (adjust the quantity depending on the softness of dates)

## Mango cheesecake filling:

2½   cups (325g) cashew nuts, soaked          2   cups chopped well-ripe mangoes

4-6  tablespoons honey or liquid sweetener of your choice (quantity depends on the sweetness of mangos)

4     tablespoons nut milk of your choice (see page 23 in the Techniques and Advance Preparation chapter) or water

2     tablespoons lemon juice          1   teaspoon vanilla extract

¼     teaspoon salt

2     tablespoons lecithin; if unavailable, it is ok to omit

230  ml coconut oil, melted if solid (for the lighter version, use 140 ml coconut oil + 120ml Irish moss paste)

## Garnish:

4     tablespoons chocolate ganache sauce (see page 53 in the Sweet Creams and Sauces chapter)

1. For the crust, in the food processor, process all the ingredients except for the dates until well ground.
2. Add dates, little by little, while processing. The consistency should be enough to be held together by hand, but still easy to break. If it is too dry, add some more dates or coconut oil.
3. Press the mixture into a lightly greased pan and set aside in the fridge.
4. For the filling, blend all ingredients except for coconut oil (and Irish moss) until smooth.
5. Add coconut oil (and Irish moss) and blend evenly.
6. Pour onto the crust and refrigerate for 8 hours or overnight until set.
7. Drizzle the chocolate ganache over the top.

# Raspberry Marble Cheesecake

Swirl makes this cheesecake not only pretty and delicious looking and makes you professional!

Yields a 8-9 inch/21-23cm cake

Blender, food processor, and 8-9 inch/21-23cm loose-bottom cake pan needed

## Crust:

¾ cup (90g) macadamia nuts

4 tablespoons cacao nibs

¾ cup (130g) deseeded dates, chopped (adjust the quantity depending on the softness of dates)

½ cup (70g) hazelnuts

¼ teaspoon salt

## Vanilla cheesecake filling:

2¾ cups (350g) cashew nuts, soaked

½ cup honey or liquid sweetener of your choice

4 tablespoons lemon juice

1 cup nut milk of your choice

¼ teaspoon salt

2 teaspoons vanilla extract

1 tablespoon lemon zest or a few drops lemon essential oil

2 tablespoons lecithin; if unavailable, it is ok to omit

160 ml coconut oil, melted if solid

70ml (60g) melted cacao butter (for the lighter version, use 100 ml coconut oil +40ml (35g) melted cacao butter + 120ml Irish moss paste)

## Raspberry cheesecake filing:

1 cup raspberries

2 tablespoons coconut oil, melted if solid

2 tablespoons honey or liquid sweetener of your choice

1. For the crust, process all the ingredients except for the dates in a food processor until well ground.
2. Add dates, little by little, while processing. The consistency should be enough to be held together by hand, but still easy to break. If it is too dry, add some more dates or coconut oil.
3. Press the mixture into a lightly greased pan and set aside in the fridge.
4. For the vanilla cheesecake filling, blend all ingredients, except for coconut oil, cacao butter (and Irish moss) until smooth.
5. Add coconut oil, cacao butter (and Irish moss) and blend evenly.
6. Take out 1/3 quantity of the filling into a bowl.
7. Add raspberry cheesecake filling into the remaining mixture in the blender, blend until smooth, then transfer into another bowl.
8. Pour the 2 kinds of filling randomly onto the crust.
9. Flatten the surface by tapping the cake on the table gently and insert a bamboo stick or chopstick into the filling vertically, draw a circle gently or move it around to create your desired pattern.(see FYI on page 107 for Orange White Chocolate Cheesecake in this chapter)
10. Refrigerate for 8 hours or overnight until set.

# Mint and Spirulina Cheesecake

How can you go wrong with mint and chocolate? This is hands-down one of my favorite cheesecakes!

Yields 8-9 inch/21-23cm cake
Blender, food processor, and 8-9 inch/21-23cm loose-bottom cake pan needed

## Crust:
1½   cups (115g) desiccated shredded coconuts

¾    cup (100g) cashew nuts

2    tablespoons cacao nibs

¼    teaspoon salt

¾    cup (130g) deseeded dates, chopped (adjust the quantity depending on the softness of dates)

## Lemon cheesecake filling:
2¾   cups (350g) cashew nuts, soaked

½    cup honey or liquid sweetener of your choice

½    cup water

4    tablespoons lemon juice

2    tablespoons lemon zest or a few drops lemon essential oil

2    teaspoons vanilla extract

¼    teaspoon salt

2    tablespoons lecithin; if unavailable, it is ok to omit

230  ml coconut oil, melted if solid (for the lighter version, use 140 ml coconut oil + 120ml Irish moss paste)

## Mint spirulina filling:
½    cup peppermint leaves, (or 1 teaspoon peppermint extract or a few drops essential oil)

1    teaspoon spirulina powder

## Chocolate swirl:
2    tablespoons cacao powder

1    tablespoon water

1. For the crust, process shredded coconuts into powder in the food processor, and then add all the ingredients except for the dates and process until well ground.

2. Add dates, little by little, while processing. The consistency should be enough to be held together by hand, but still easy to break. If it is too dry, add some more dates or coconut oil.

3. Press the mixture into a lightly greased pan and set aside in the fridge.

4. For the lemon cheesecake filling, blend all ingredients except for coconut oil (and Irish moss) until smooth.

5. Add coconut oil (and Irish moss) and blend evenly.

6. Pour half of the filling onto the crust and place in the freezer to set for 30 minutes.

7. Add mint spirulina filling into the remaining mixture in the blender, blend until smooth, then pour on top of the lemon cheesecake filling, saving ½ cup of filling for the chocolate swirl.

8. Transfer the saved ½ cup filling, add all the chocolate swirl ingredients, mix until well incorporated, then transfer into a squeeze bottle.

9. Drop the dots of chocolate mixture onto the filling, flatten the surface by tapping the cake onto the table gently and insert a bamboo stick or chopstick into the filling vertically, draw the circle gently or move it around to create your desired pattern. (See FYI on page 107 for Orange White Chocolate Cheesecake in this chapter)

10. Refrigerate for 8 hours or overnight until set.

# "Oreo" Cream Cheesecake

Even though I'd been far away from commercial "oreo" cookies, I still remember its perfect combination of bitter biscuit and rich creamy filling. One day, I was in need to manifest it. We all need its luxury in our life! Cheesecake is awesome and life is good ;)

Yields 8-9 inch/21-23cm size cake
Blender, food processor and 8-9 inch/21-23cm bottom-removal cake mold needed

## "Oreo" crust and topping:
1½   cups cacao nibs

½    cup finely ground coconut sugar or any natural powder sugar; if unavailable, use 1 cup (170g) chopped dates

¼    teaspoon salt

5    tablespoons coconut oil, melted of solid

## White cream cheesecake filling:
2¼   cups (300g) cashew nuts, soaked

1    cup water

½    cup + 2 tablespoons honey or liquid sweetener of your choice

4    tablespoons lemon juice

2    teaspoons vanilla extract

¼    teaspoon salt

1    tablespoon lecithin; if unavailable, it is ok to omit

90   ml coconut oil, melted if solid

160  ml (140g) melted cacao butter

1. For the "oreo" crust, in the food processor, grind cacao nibs, coconut sugar and salt into fine powder. (If you are using dates, ground cacao nibs and salt into powder first, and then add dates to process evenly.)
2. Add coconut oil and process evenly.
3. Press half of the mixture into a lightly greased pan and set aside in the fridge. (keep the rest of the half "oreo" crust in the room temperature.)
4. For the white cream cheesecake filling, blend all ingredients except for coconut oil and cacao butter until smooth.
5. Add coconut oil and cacao butter and blend evenly.
6. Pour onto the "oreo" crust and place in the freezer to set for 30 minutes.
7. Take the cake out of freezer, cover the cake surface with the remaining "oreo" crumble, and then refrigerate for 4-6 hours or until set.

## Variations:

### Strawberry "Oreo" Cream Cheesecake
Reduce the quantity of lemon juice into 2 tablespoons, and add 1½ cups fresh strawberries in the filling and blend, and then 1 cup halved strawberries at the end to fold in.

### Mint & Spirulina "Oreo" Cream Cheesecake
Add 2 teaspoons spirulina powder and ½ cup peppermint leaves or 1 teaspoon peppermint extract or a few drops essential oil (and 2 teaspoons any green powder) in the filling and blend.

### Moringa Mint Chocolate Chip "Oreo" Cream Cheesecake
Add 2 teaspoons moringa powder (see FYI below) and ½ cup peppermint leaves or 1 teaspoon peppermint extract or a few drops essential oil (and 2 teaspoons any green powder) in the filling and blend, and then ½ cup roughly chopped dark chocolate at the end to fold in.

**FYI:** For moringa, see page 159 in the Moringa Mint Chocolate Chip Ice Cream in Ice Cream chapter

# Passion Cheesecake

I think passion fruits is the best fruits for cheesecake. It is such an amazing fruity flavorful sweet & tanginess merges perfectly into the rich creamy cheesecake.

Yields 8-9 inch/21-23cm size cake
Blender, food processor and 8-9 inch/21-23cm bottom-removal cake mold needed

## Crust:
1    cup nut flour ([see page 24](#) in the Techniques and Advance Preparation chapter)

½    cup (70g) almonds

1½   tablespoons cacao nibs

¼    teaspoon salt

3    tablespoons maple syrup or liquid sweetener of your choice

2    tablespoons coconut oil, melted of solid

## Passion fruits cheesecake filling:
2½   cups (325g) cashew nuts, soaked

1    cup yellow (sour-type) passion fruits pulp (may need around 8-10 pieces of passion fruits)

½    cup +2 tablespoons honey or liquid sweetener of your choice

½    cup water

1    teaspoon vanilla extract

¼    teaspoon salt

1    tablespoon lecithin; if unavailable, it is ok to omit

170  ml coconut oil, melted of solid

⅓    cup (70g) melted cacao butter

## Passion fruits jelly:
½    cup yellow (sour-type) passion fruits pup (may need around 4 pieces of passion fruits)

1    cup soaked Irish moss ([see page 30](#) in the Techniques and Advance Preparation chapter)

1    cup water

3-4  tablespoons honey or liquid sweetener of your choice

3    tablespoons coconut oil, melted of solid

1    teaspoon psyllium husk

1. For the crust, in the food processor, process almond first into powder, then add nut flour, cacao nibs and salt to process into powder, and then add maple syrup and coconut oil while processing. The consistency should be easily to hold together by hand. If it is too dry, add a little liquid ingredient to adjust the consistency.
2. Press the mixture into a lightly greased pan and set aside in the fridge.
3. For passion fruits cheesecake filling, blend all ingredients except for coconut oil and cacao butter until smooth.
4. Add coconut oil and cacao butter and blend evenly.
5. Pour onto the crust and place in the freezer to set while making passion fruits jelly.
6. For the passion fruits jelly, blend soaked Irish moss and water until slight warm and Irish moss is completely dissolved, transfer into a bowl, add all the rest ingredient and mix with the whisk until smooth.
7. Take the cake out of freezer and make sure it is completely set. If not, place back in the freezer until it sets for another 1 hour. (While waiting for the cake to set, do not refrigerate the jelly to avoid hardening.)
8. Spread the jelly on top gently and then refrigerate for 4-6 hours or until set.

# Banana Caramel Cheesecake

Easy, never-failing dessert that makes everyone happy and smile :)

Yields 8-9 inch/21-23cm size cake
Blender, food processor and 8-9 inch/21-23cm bottom-removal cake mold needed

## Crust:

| | |
|---|---|
| ¾ cup (90g) walnuts | ¾ cup (100g) cashew nuts |
| 2 tablespoons cacao nibs | ¼ teaspoon salt |

¾ cup (130g) deseeded dates, chopped (adjust the quantity depending on the softness of dates)

## Banana caramel cheesecake filling:

| | |
|---|---|
| 2½ cups (325g) cashew nuts, soaked | 1½ cups banana, chopped |

1 cup nut milk of your choice (see page 23 in the Techniques and Advance Preparation chapter) or water

| | |
|---|---|
| ½ cup maple syrup | 3 tablespoons lemon juice |
| 1 teaspoon vanilla extract | ¼ teaspoon salt |

5-6 drops medicine flower's caramel extract (optional) (see page 18 in the Staple Ingredients and Raw Alternatives chapter)

2 tablespoons lecithin; if unavailable, it is ok to omit

230 ml coconut oil, melted if solid (for the lighter version, use 140 ml coconut oil + 120ml Irish moss paste)

## Salted caramel sauce:

| | |
|---|---|
| 2 tablespoons tahini or almond butter | 2 tablespoons maple syrup |
| 2 tablespoons coconut oil, melted if solid, | 1 teaspoons vanilla extract |
| ⅛ teaspoon salt | |

1. For the crust, in the food processor, process all the ingredients except for the dates until well ground.
2. Add dates, little by little, while processing. The consistency should be enough to be held together by hand, but still easy to break. If it is too dry, add some more dates or coconut oil.
3. Press the mixture into a lightly greased pan and set aside in the fridge.
4. For the banana caramel cheesecake filling, blend all ingredients except for coconut oil (and Irish moss) until smooth.
5. Add coconut oil (and Irish moss) and blend evenly.
6. Pour onto the crust and refrigerate for 8 hours or overnight until set.
7. For the salted caramel sauce, mix all ingredients in a bowl with the whisk until smooth, and then transfer into a small-nozzle squeeze bottle.
8. To garnish, take the cake out of the pan, and drizzle the salted caramel sauce on top.

# Chai Persimmon Cheesecake

Chai flavor merged into persimmon ⋯ what a treat!

Yields  8-9 inch/21-23cm cake
Blender, food processor, and 8-9 inch/21-23cm loose-bottom cake pan needed

## Crust:

| | | | |
|---|---|---|---|
| 1 | cup (75g) desiccated shredded coconut | 1 | cup (140g) almonds |
| 2 | tablespoons cacao nibs | 1 | teaspoon cinnamon powder |
| ¼ | teaspoon cardamom powder | ¼ | teaspoon salt |

¾  cup (130g) deseeded dates chopped (adjust the quantity depending on the softness of dates)

## Persimmon cheesecake filling:

2½  cups (325g) cashew nuts, soaked

2  cups chopped well-ripe persimmon (about 2 large persimmons)

4-8  tablespoons honey or liquid sweetener of your choice (quantity depends on the sweetness of persimmons)

4  tablespoons nut milk of your choice (see page 23 in the Techniques and Advance Preparation chapter) or water

3  tablespoons lemon juice

2  teaspoons vanilla extract

¼  teaspoon salt

2  tablespoons lecithin; if unavailable, it is ok to omit

230  ml coconut oil, melted if solid

2  tablespoons (26g) melted cacao butter (for the lighter version, use 150 ml coconut oil + 1 tablespoon cacao butter + 120ml Irish moss paste)

## Chai swirl:

2  teaspoons chai spices
(or 1½ teaspoon cinnamon powder + ½ teaspoon cardamom powder + ½ teaspoon ginger powder + pinch of clove powder)

1½  tablespoons cacao powder

1  tablespoons coconut oil, melted if solid

1  tablespoon water

1. For the crust, process shredded coconut into powder in the food processor, then add all the ingredients except for the dates and process until well ground.
2. Add dates, little by little, while processing. The consistency should be enough to be held together by hand, but still easy to break. If it is too dry, add some more dates or coconut oil.
3. Press the mixture into a lightly greased pan and set aside in the fridge.
4. For the persimmon cheesecake filling, blend all ingredients except for coconut oil, cacao butter (and Irish moss) until smooth.
5. Add coconut oil, cacao butter (and Irish moss) and blend evenly.
6. Pour onto the crust, saving 1 1/2 cups of filling for the chai swirl.
7. Add the chai swirl ingredients to the remaining filling and blend until smooth and transfer into the squeeze bottle.
8. Drop the dots of chai mixture onto the filling, flatten the surface by tapping the cake onto the table gently, and insert a bamboo stick or chopstick into the filling vertically, draw the circle gently or move it around to create your desired pattern. (see FYI on page 107 for Orange White Chocolate Cheesecake below in this chapter)
9. Refrigerate for 8 hours or overnight until set.

# Orange White Chocolate Cheesecake

Velvety white chocolate and fresh tangy orange are perfect together!

Yields 8-9 inch/21-23cm cake

Blender, food processor, and 8-9 inch/21-23cm loose-bottom cake pan needed

## Crust:

| | | | |
|---|---|---|---|
| 1 | cup (75g) desiccated shredded coconut | 1 | cup (140g) almonds |
| 1 | teaspoon cinnamon powder | ¼ | teaspoon salt |
| ¾ | cup (130g) deseeded dates, chopped (adjust the quantity depending on softness of dates) | | |

## Orange white chocolate cheesecake filling:

| | | | |
|---|---|---|---|
| 2¾ | cups (350g) cashew nuts, soaked | 2 | cups orange juice |
| ½ | cup honey or liquid sweetener of your choice | 3 | tablespoons lemon juice |
| 1 | tablespoon orange zest or a few drops orange essential oil | | |
| 2 | tablespoons lecithin; if unavailable, it is ok to omit | | |
| ¼ | teaspoon salt | | |
| 160 | ml coconut oil, melted if solid | | |
| 70 | ml (60g) melted cacao butter (for the lighter version, use 100 ml coconut oil +40ml (35g) melted cacao butter + 120ml Irish moss paste) | | |

## Chocolate swirl:

| | | | |
|---|---|---|---|
| 2 | tablespoons cacao powder | 1 | tablespoon water |

1. For the procedure, follow the directions for Chai Persimmon Cheesecake (see the recipe on page 104 in this chapter)

### FYI: How to Create Swirl Pattern

1. Make sure that both the filling and swirl mixtures' consistencies are similar, that is the key to create the beautiful swirl pattern.

2. Prepare the swirl mixture in the squeezing bottle, which makes it easy to create the perfect dots.

3. Make small and large dots in the surface of the filling to create an interesting swirl. If you pierce the nozzle of the squeeze bottle deep into the filling and squeeze with higher pressure, it will make the pattern inside of the filling as well, so that you will see the beautiful pattern when you cut the cake.

4. If you squeeze with lighter pressure on top of the surface, it only makes a pattern on the surface.

5. Using the both techniques, make a variety of multiple-sized dots.

6. If you have more than you need for the swirl, then you do not have to use it all.

7. Flatten the surface by tapping the cake onto the table gently.

8. Now insert a bamboo stick or chopstick into the filling vertically, draw a circle gently or move it around to create your desired pattern.

# TARTS AND PIES

Raw tarts and pies are not only tastier, but they are actually so much easier than baked ones.

# Fruit Tart in Season

Best way to enjoy the fruits in season!

Yields 9 inch/23cm tart
Blender, food processor, and 9 inch/23cm loose-bottom tart pan needed

## Crust:
1    cup (140g) almonds

1    cup (120g) walnuts

¼    teaspoon salt

2    tablespoons maple syrup

## Lemon cream filling:
2    cups (260g) cashew nuts, soaked

6     tablespoons (80ml) honey or liquid sweetener of your choice

4    tablespoons lemon juice

4    tablespoons water

1    tablespoon lemon zest or a few drops lemon essential oil

1    teaspoon vanilla extract

¼    teaspoon salt

6     tablespoons (80ml) coconut oil, melted if solid

## Topping:
3    cups seasonal fruit of your choice

1. For the crust, process almonds into powder in the food processor, then add walnuts and salt and process until well ground.
2. Add maple syrup while processing. The consistency should be enough to be held together by hand, but still easy to break. If it is too dry, add a little more maple syrup or coconut oil.
3. Press the mixture into the lightly greased pan and trim the rim of the pan, then set aside in the fridge.
4. For the lemon cream filling, blend all ingredients until smooth.
5. Pour onto the crust evenly and decorate with the fruit on top.
6. Refrigerate for a couple of hours or overnight until set.

# Double Chocolate Pie

Today is a gift, let's celebrate with the "present" of a chocolate pie!

Yields 9 inch/23cm pie
Blender, food processor, and 9 inch/23cm loose-bottom pie pan needed

## Hazelnut crust:

1     cup hazelnuts (140g)

½    cup cashew nuts (65g)

2     tablespoons cacao powder

2     tablespoons cacao nibs

¼    teaspoon salt

¾-1 cup (130-170g) deseeded dates, chopped (adjust the quantity depending on the softness of dates)

## Chocolate filling:

2     cups (260g) cashew nuts, soaked

1     cup date paste (see page 31 in the Techniques and Advance Preparation chapter)

1     cup water

½    cup coconut oil, melted if solid

2     tablespoons maple syrup

1     teaspoon vanilla extract

¼    teaspoon salt

1     cup cacao powder

1. For the crust, process all the ingredients except for the dates in the food processor until well ground.
2. Add dates, little by little, while processing. The consistency should be enough to be held together by hand, but still easy to break. If it is too dry, add some more dates or coconut oil.
3. Press the mixture into the lightly greased pan and trim the rim of the pan, then set aside in the fridge.
4. For the chocolate filling, blend all ingredients except for cacao powder until smooth.
5. Add cacao powder and blend until well incorporated.
6. Pour onto the crust evenly, and smoothen the surface.
7. Refrigerate for a couple of hours or overnight until set.

# Banana Dream Pie

Tomorrow is unknown, eat dessert now!

Yields 9 inch/23cm pie
Blender, food processor, and 9 inch/23cm loose-bottom pie pan needed

## Crust:
1    cup (75g) desiccated shredded coconut

1    cup + 2 tablespoons (145g) cashew nuts

¼    teaspoon salt

¾-1 cup (130~170g) deseeded dates, chopped  (adjust the quantity depending on  softness of dates)

2    tablespoons cacao nibs

2    tablespoons cacao powder

## Mango custard cream:
1    cup chopped mango

½    cup coconut oil, melted if solid

4    tablespoons honey or liquid sweetener of your choice

1    tablespoon lemon zest or a few drops lemon essential oil

1    cup (130g) cashew nuts, soaked

## Assembly:
2    cups Vanilla Whippy Cream (see page 51 in the Sweet Creams and Sauces chapter)

6-7  bananas

Maca caramel sauce and chocolate ganache sauce (see page 53 in the Sweet Creams and Sauces chapter) as desired (optional)

1. For the crust, process desiccated coconut into powder in the food processor, then add all the rest of the ingredients except for the dates and process until well ground.
2. Add dates, little by little, while processing. The consistency should be enough to be held together by hand, but still easy to break. If it is too dry, add some more dates or coconut oil.
3. Press the mixture into the lightly greased pan and trim the rim of the pan, then set aside in the fridge.
4. For the mango custard cream, blend all ingredients until smooth.
5. Pour onto the crust evenly, lay the whole bananas on it, press the bananas into the mango custard cream so that the cream in between bananas rises up to fill up the space, then set aside in the freezer to set for about 30 minutes to1 hour.
6. Place the vanilla whippy cream on top, and create the round dome shape.
7. Refrigerate for 8 hours or overnight until set.
8. Drizzle maca caramel sauce and chocolate ganache sauce to garnish if desired.

# Coconut Merengue Pie

So light and absolutely gorgeous!! Irish moss is the key for the light heavenly texture.

Yields 9 inch/23cm pie
Blender, food processor, and 9 inch/23cm loose-bottom pie pan needed

## Crust:

1½    cups (180g) macadamia nuts

1      cup (75g) desiccated shredded coconut

¼      teaspoon salt

100   ml (70g) deseeded dates, chopped (adjust the quantity depending on the softness of dates)

## Lemon cream filling:

½      cup well-packed soaked Irish moss (see page 30 in the Techniques and Advance Preparation chapter)

½      cup lemon juice

1      cup (130g) cashew nuts, soaked

½      cup + 2 tablespoons honey or liquid sweetener of your choice

       pinch salt

1      tablespoon lemon zest or a few drops lemon essential oil

1      teaspoon pumpkin powder or pinch turmeric powder (optional for coloring)

2      tablespoons lecithin

½      cup + 2 tablespoons coconut oil, melted if solid

## Coconut merengue:

1      cup well-packed soaked Irish moss (see page 30 in the Techniques and Advance Preparation chapter)

2      cups coconut milk (see page 23 in the Techniques and Advance Preparation chapter); if unavailable, use any nut milk

1½    cups medium soft coconut meat from young coconut; if unavailable, use soaked cashew nuts

⅓      cup honey or liquid sweetener of your choice

2      teaspoons vanilla extract

2      teaspoons lemon juice

       pinch salt

2      tablespoons lecithin

½      cup +2 tablespoons coconut oil, melded if solid

1. For the crust, process desiccated coconut into powder in the food processor, then add all the rest of the ingredients except for the dates and process until well ground.

2. Add dates, little by little, while processing. The consistency should be enough to be held together by hand, but still easy to break. If it is too dry, add some more dates or coconut oil.

3. Press the mixture into the lightly greased pan and trim the rim of the pan, then set aside in the fridge.

4. For the lemon cream filling, first blend soaked Irish moss and lemon juice until slightly warm and the Irish moss is completely dissolved, then transfer into a bowl and set aside.

5. Blend all the rest of the ingredients except for coconut oil until smooth.

6. Add Irish moss mixture and coconut oil, and blend until well incorporated.

7. Pour onto the crust evenly and refrigerate for a couple of hours (or freeze for 1 hour) or until set.

8. For the coconut merengue, first blend soaked Irish moss and 1 cup of coconut milk until slightly warm and Irish moss is completely dissolved, then transfer into a bowl and set aside.

9. Blend all the rest of the ingredients except for coconut oil until smooth.

10. Add Irish moss mixture and coconut oil and blend until well incorporated.

11. Transfer into the large flat container so that it will set quicker and refrigerate for a few hour or until set.

12. When the coconut merengue is well-set, smoothen with a whippier, place onto the lemon cream filling evenly and create the "merengue- peak" using the back of the spoon or offset spatula. (Place the back of the spoon on the merengue gently, pick it up vertically, and continue this process to cover the surface.)

13. Refrigerate for another few hours to set.

**FYI:** 600g fresh pumpkin yields roughly about 1 ½ cups dehydrated pumpkin, although it depends on its dryness. To make dehydrated Pumpkin, thickly slice the fresh pumpkin and dehydrate overnight on the mesh screen.

# Pumpkin Pie

Although it takes a bit of preparation, it is absolutely worth it! Tastes like a traditional old-fashioned grandma's pumpkin pie!

Yields 9 inch/23cm pie
Blender, food processor, dehydrator, and 9 inch/23cm loose-bottom pie pan needed

## Pecan crust:

¾ cup (105g) almonds

1 cup (120g) pecan nuts

1 teaspoon cinnamon powder

¼ teaspoon salt

¾-1 cup (130~170g) deseeded dates, chopped (adjust the quantity depending on softness of dates)

## Pumpkin cream filling:

1½ cups dried pumpkin, soaked in water for a few hours (see FYI on page to left)

½ cup water

2 cups (130g) cashew nuts, soaked

1 cup coconut oil, melted if solid

½ cup maple syrup

⅓ cup (70g) melted cacao butter

1 teaspoon vanilla extract

1 teaspoon cinnamon powder

¼ teaspoon nutmeg powder

¼ teaspoon salt

## Garnish:

½ tablespoon each goji berries and pumpkin seeds, or any nuts and dried fruits of your choice

1. For the crust, process almonds into powder in the food processor, then add all the rest of the ingredients except for dates and process until well ground.
2. Add dates, little by little, while processing. The consistency should be enough to be held together by hand, but still easy to break. If it is too dry, add some more dates or coconut oil.
3. Press the mixture into the lightly greased pan and trim the rim of the pan, then set aside in the fridge.
4. For the pumpkin cream filling, blend pumpkin and water until completely smooth and set aside in a bowl. If the mixture is too dense to blend, add some coconut oil (from the recipe ingredients) to facilitate easy blending.
5. Blend all the rest of the ingredients until smooth (if some coconut oil was used for blending the pumpkin, reduce the amount).
6. Transfer into the pumpkin mixture bowl and mix with whisk until evenly combined.
7. Transfer into a flat container and refrigerate for 30 minutes to1 hour.
8. Pour half of the filling onto the crust and refrigerate the remaining filling for a few hours to set.
9. When the filling is well-set, transfer the filling into a piping bag with star (or any shape) nozzle and squeeze on top to decorate, garnish with goji berries and pumpkin seeds.
10. Refrigerate for another few hours until set.

# Banoffee Pie

English tradition recreated in delicious raw! It is a rich creamy pie made from bananas, cream, and toffee.

Yields 9 inch/23cm pie, Blender, food processor, and 9 inch/23cm loose-bottom pie pan needed

## Crust:

¾ cup (105g) hazelnut ½ cup (65g) cashew nuts

¾ cup coconut flour (dried, powdered nut pulp, see page 24 in the Techniques and Advance Preparation chapter)

¾ cup ground hazelnut (hazelnut powder) (see page 25 in the Techniques and Advance Preparation chapter for grinding)

1 teaspoon vanilla extract ¼ teaspoon salt

¼ cup (43g) deseeded dates, chopped 1½ tablespoons maple syrup

1½ tablespoons coconut oil, melted if solid

## Toffee cream filling:

1 cup (170g) deseeded dates, chopped and soaked in 6 tablespoons water for 30 minutes

½ cup (120g) coconut butter; if unavailable, use almond butter or tahini

4 tablespoons maple syrup 2 tablespoons lucuma power

4 tablespoons coconut oil, melted if solid 2 teaspoons vanilla extract

½ teaspoon salt

10 drops medicine flower's butterscotch or caramel extract (optional) (see page 18 in the Staple Ingredients and Raw Alternatives chapter)

## Assembly:

3 cups (1.5 times of the recipe) Vanilla Whippy Cream (see page 51 in the Sweet Creams and Sauces chapter)

4–5 bananas, sliced into halves lengthwise

1 piece of dark chocolate (see page 133 in the Chocolate chapter), grated

1. For the crust, in the food processor, process hazel nuts and cashew nuts first into powder, then add nut flour, vanilla extract and salt to process into powder.

2. Add dates, little by little, while processing, and then add maple syrup and coconut oil while processing. The consistency should be easily to hold together by hand. If it is too dry, add a little liquid ingredient to adjust the consistency.

3. Press the mixture into the lightly greased pan and trim the rim of the pan, then set aside in the fridge.

4. For the toffee cream filling, blend dates, including the soaking water, and maple syrup in the blender until smooth, add all the rest of the ingredients and blend until smooth, and pour onto the crust.

5. Place the sliced bananas onto the toffee cream facing the cut edge on the bottom and refrigerate for about 1 hour to set.

6. Transfer the vanilla whippy cream into a piping bag with a round nozzle and squeeze on top to decorate, and sprinkle with some grated chocolate for garnish.

7. Refrigerate for a couple hours or overnight until set.

# Key Lime Coconut Pie

Nice and tart, creamy pie is made with **avocado**! Surprise your friends!

Yields 9 inch/23cm pie
Blender, food processor, and 9 inch/23cm loose-bottom pie pan needed

## Crust:

| | | | |
|---|---|---|---|
| 1 | cup (75g) desiccated shredded coconut | 1 | cup (140g) almonds |
| ¼ | teaspoon salt | | |

¾-1 cup (130~170g) deseeded dates, chopped (adjust the quantity depending on softness of dates)

## Key lime cream filling:

3 cups chopped well-ripe avocado (about 2 large avocados)
½ cup coconut oil, melded if solid
½ cup + 2 tablespoons honey or liquid sweetener of your choice
⅓ cup lime juice
4 tablespoons (55g) melted cacao butter
1 tablespoon lime zest or a few drops lime essential oil
2 teaspoons vanilla extract
½ cup Irish moss paste (see page 31 in the Techniques and Advance Preparation chapter)
1 tablespoon lecithin

## Garnish: (see FYI below)
1½ cups freshly grated mature coconut; if unavailable, use desicated coconut
Slices of lime as desired

1. For the crust, process coconut into powder in the food processor, then add all the rest of the ingredients except for the dates and process until well ground.
2. Add dates, little by little, while processing. The consistency should be enough to be held together by hand, but still easy to break. If it is too dry, add some more dates or coconut oil.
3. Press the mixture into the lightly greased pan and trim the rim of the pan, then set aside in the fridge.
4. For the key lime cream filling, blend all ingredients except for Irish moss paste until smooth.
5. Add Irish moss paste and blend until well incorporated.
6. Pour onto the crust evenly and refrigerate for 8 hours or overnight until set.
7. Decorate with grated coconut and lime slices.

**FYI:** Another idea for garnish on top is coconut merengue (see page 114 for Coconut Merengue Pie recipe in this chapter) or Vanilla Whippy Cream (see page 51 in the Sweet Creams and Sauces chapter).

# COOKIES AND BISCUITS

Even if you do not have a dehydrator, you don't have to give up cookies! You can simply refrigerate them and they will be nice and hard when chilled.

# Almond Butter Cookies with Apricot Jam Dot

"Butter" and jam … an irresistible combination!

Yields 20 pieces of 2 inch/5cm diameter cookies          food processor and dehydrator needed

## Almond butter cookies:

2     cups nut pulp (see page 24 in the Techniques and Advance Preparation chapter)(if using nut flour, add some more water to adjust the consistency)

½     cup date paste (see page 31 in the Techniques and Advance Preparation chapter)

½     cup coconut oil, melted if solid

½     cup (120g) almond butter

4     tablespoons ground flaxseeds (see page 25 in the Techniques and Advance Preparation chapter for grinding)

4     tablespoons water

1     teaspoon vanilla extract

¼     teaspoon salt

## Apricot jam:

½     cup apricot jam (apricot jam can be made in the same way as date paste, see page 31 in the Techniques and Advance Preparation chapter for date paste)

1. For the almond butter cookies, mix all ingredients in a bowl by hand until well incorporated.
2. Roll into golf-ball sizes (about 1.2 inch/3cm diameter), and then flatten into 2 inch/5cm round shapes.
3. Make the thumbprint indention and fill it with apricot jam.
4. Place onto the mesh screen, dehydrate at 105-115 ° F/41-46 ° C overnight or until dry outside but soft inside.

# Chocolate Biscuits

My childhood favorite comes back in raw!

Yields15 of 2.4 inch/6cm round cookies          dehydrator and cookie cutter (optional)  needed

1     cup nut pulp (see page 24 in the Techniques and Advance Preparation chapter)(if using nut flour, add some water to adjust the consistency)

¼     cup (38g) ground almond (almond powder) (see page 24 in the Techniques and Advance Preparation chapter for grinding)

½     cup date paste (see page 31 in the Techniques and Advance Preparation chapter)

½     cup cacao powder

2     tablespoons maple syrup

1     teaspoon vanilla extract

¼     teaspoon salt

½     cup (70g) chopped walnuts

1. Combine all ingredients in a bowl except for walnuts and mix by hand until well incorporated.
2. Roll the mixture (using the plastic wrap so that it doesn't stick to the board) into 0.3 inch/0.8cm thick.
3. Remove the plastic wrap on top, sprinkle with walnuts evenly and roll again tightly to press the walnuts into the dough.
4. Cut into your favorite shapes using a cookie cutter. If a cookies cutter is unavailable, cut into your favorite shapes using a knife.
5. Place onto the mesh screen, dehydrate at 105-115° F/41-46° C overnight or until dry outside.

# Marzipan Shortbreads with Chocolate & Salted Caramel Drizzle

I love its delicate crumbly texture of marzipan! Aren't they adorable? It's best to keep in the freezer because of the coconut oil in the chocolate sauce.

Yields 12-16 shortbreads
Blender, food processor and 9inch/23cm round tart pan or 8.3x8.3inch/21x21cm square pan needed

## Marzipan shortbreads:
| | |
|---|---|
| 1 | cup (240g) almond butter |
| 4 | tablespoons maple syrup or liquid sweetener of your choice |
| 4 | tablespoons coconut oil, melted of solid |
| ¼ | teaspoon almond extract or a few drops medicine flower's almond extract (optional) (see page 18 in the Staple Ingredients and Raw Alternatives chapter) |
| ⅛ | teaspoon salt |
| 1 | cup nut flour (see page 24 in the Techniques and Advance Preparation chapter) |

## Chocolate sauce:
| | |
|---|---|
| 8 | tablespoons coconut oil, melted of solid |
| 4 | tablespoons maple syrup or liquid sweetener of your choice |
| ⅛ | teaspoon salt |
| 4 | tablespoons cacao powder |

## Salted caramel sauce:
| | |
|---|---|
| 2 | tablespoons any "butter" such as tahini, almond butter or coconut butter |
| 2 | tablespoons coconut oil, melted of solid |
| 2 | tablespoons maple syrup |
| ½ | teaspoon vanilla extract |
| | a few drops medicine flower's caramel extract (optional) (see page 18 in the Staple Ingredients and Raw Alternatives chapter) |
| ⅛ | teaspoon salt |

## Topping:
1-2 tablespoons chopped nuts or cacao nibs (optional)

1. Lightly grease the pan then line with parchment paper on the bottom.
2. For the marzipan shortbreads, process all ingredients except for nut flour in the food processor until evenly blended, add nut flour and process evenly. The consistency should be easily to hold together by hand. If it is too dry, add a little liquid ingredient to adjust the consistency.
3. Transfer into the pan and press down firmly, then place in the freezer while making the chocolate sauce.
4. For the chocolate sauce, blend all ingredients, pour it over the marzipan evenly, and then place in the freezer while making the salted caramel sauce.
5. For the salted caramel sauce, blend all ingredients, transfer into a small-nozzle squeeze bottle, drizzle over the top, then garnish with some chopped nuts or cacao nibs if desired.
6. Freeze for half an hour before cutting into 12-16 pieces to serve.

# Macadamia and White Chocolate Drop Cookies

This reminds me those conventional cookies that I'd been addicted to for long time :)

Yields 10 of 3 inch/8cm cookies                                    dehydrator needed

1½  cups nut pulp (see page 24 in the Techniques and Advance Preparation chapter) (if using nut flour, add some water to adjust the consistency)

1½  cups (240g) ground cashew nuts (see page 25 in the Techniques and Advance Preparation chapter for grinding)

6    tablespoons maple syrup

1    teaspoon vanilla extract

¼    teaspoon salt

1    cup (250g) Vanilla White Chocolate Fudge (see page 139 in Chocolates chapter), large chunked and kept in the fridge

1    cup (120g) macadamia nuts, cut into halves

1. Combine all ingredients in a bowl except for vanilla white chocolate fudge and macadamia nuts and mix by hand until well incorporated.
2. Fold in vanilla white chocolate fudge and macadamia nuts.
3. Roll into 2 inch/5cm diameter balls and flatten onto the nonstick sheet into 3 inch/8cm round pieces.
4. Dehydrate at 105-115° F/41-46° C for a couple of hours, then transfer onto the mesh screen, continue to dehydrate for 8 hours or until dry outside but soft inside.

# Chocolate-Covered Vanilla Cookies

This is the result of "I-wanna-cover-everything-with-chocolate" symptom.

Yields 15 pieces of 1.6x4 inch/4x10cm cookies                    dehydrator needed

2½  cups (400g) ground cashew nuts (see page 25 in the Techniques and Advance Preparation chapter for grinding)

1¾  cups nut flour (see page 24 in the Techniques and Advance Preparation chapter)(if using nut pulp, reduce water quantity to adjust the consistency)

⅔   cup coconut sugar syrup or maple syrup

1½  teaspoons cinnamon powder

1    teaspoon vanilla extract

½   teaspoon salt

¼   cup water

½   cup chopped nuts of any kind

## Coating:

1¼  cups (300g) melted dark chocolate (see page 133 for Chocolates chapter)

1. Combine all ingredients in a bowl except for the chopped nuts and mix by hand until well incorporated.
2. Roll the mixture (using the plastic warp so that it doesn' t stick to the board) into 0.2 inch/0.6cm thick.
3. Remove the plastic wrap on top, sprinkle with chopped nuts evenly and roll again tightly to press the nuts into the dough.
4. Cut into 1.6x4 inch/4x10cm squares or your favorite shapes.
5. Place onto the mesh screen, dehydrate at 105-115°F/41-46°C overnight or until dry.
6. Dip 1 at one time into the chocolate, scoop it out using a fork, drip off the excess chocolate gently and place onto the nonstick sheet or wrap.
7. Refrigerate until set.

# CHOCOLATES

Raw chocolate is a magical food to open our heart!
Guilt-free and packed with amazing nutritional properties!

# Dark, Milk, and White Chocolate

It ensures you feel happy, sexy, and blissful! Chocolate is such a deep field, which you can write a whole book on it but here I introduce some of the easy technic you can make at home.

# EZ Dark Chocolate

For kids & chocolate beginners! Chocolate without tempering chocolate – super easy to make!

Yields 2 cups of mixture                                chocolate mold or ice cube tray needed

250 g grated cacao butter                   170  g cacao powder

80   g liquid sweetener                      ⅛   teaspoon salt

1. Place cacao butter in a bowl and warm over a double boiler and melt it completely.
2. Add the sifted cacao powder and mix until well incorporated.
3. Add all the rest of the ingredients and mix until well incorporated. (Make sure the sweetener is not cold, to avoid seizing cacao butter.)
4. Pour into the chocolate mold and refrigerate until completely sets.

# Serious Dark Chocolate

Once you master the easy chocolate making, it's time to try the tempering process! There are many ways but here we use the powdered sugar and make it finer by using the high-power blender.

Yields 2 cups of mixture        high power blender, chocolate mold and thermometer needed

250  g finely grated cacao butter

100  g powdered sweetener (blended into powder in the blender) such as coconut sugar

⅛    teaspoon salt

170  g cacao powder

1. Place the cacao butter first in the blender followed by powdered sweetener and salt. (In case the cacao butter is very cold, warm over a double boiler and melt it only about 30 % of it).
2. Blend, at a high speed, using the tamper (if you are using Vita-mix) to scrape down the mixture coming up from the sides until it becomes like a cookie dough consistency.
3. Stop the blender, scrape down all the mixture with spatula, and then once again blend at a high speed.
4. When the mixture is just about turning into liquid consistency, add the cacao powder quickly and blend a little bit until evenly blended.
5. Now, we are aiming to bring the temperature up to 108° F/42° C - the first-stage tempering temperature - by creating the heat by blending, so lets check the temperature here!

6. If it is below 108° F/42° C, blend 10 seconds at time and check the temperature every time and eventually bring up to 108° F/42° C. (Although the traditional chocolate tempering is 113° F/45° C ~122° F/ 50° C, we keep within 108° F/42° C~115° F/46° C for the 1st stage for the raw chocolate!)

7. Then bring it down to 89° F/31° C by stirring constantly in a large bowl or by spreading the chocolate onto the stainless steel or marble surface. If the room temperature is hot, place the bowl over the cold water to cool down but pay attention not to over-cooling.

8. When the temperature reaches 89° F/31° C, tempering is done!

9. Pour into the chocolate mold and refrigerate for about 20-30 minutes to set, or leave it in the room temperature if the room temperature is cool, or leave it in the air-conditioned room until it completely sets.

10. Chocolate shrinks a bit if the tempering is successful, which makes it easy to take out from the mold.

FYI: This is the easiest tempering process. In general, after the first melting stage, bring to 80.6° F /27° C ~ 84.2° F /29° C, then up to 89° F/31° C, which is also good (but more process ;) if you are using this technic, just make sure not to overheat above 91.4° F/33° C on the 3rd stage! If it goes over 91.4° F/33° C, unfortunately you need to do the tempering process again! It's testing your patience ;)

# Milk Chocolate

Yields 2 cups of mixture
high power blender, chocolate mold and thermometer needed

250  g finely grated cacao butter

60  g cashew nuts

100  g powdered sweetener (blended into powder in the blender) such as coconut sugar

⅛  teaspoon salt

100  g cacao powder

2  tablespoons lucuma powder

1. Place the cacao butter first in the blender followed by cashew nut, powdered sweetener and salt. (In case the cacao butter is very cold, warm over a double boiler and melt it only about 30 % of it).

2. Follow the "Serious Dark Chocolate" recipe process above. (Add lucuma powder together with cacao powder.)

FYI: Raw cacao is, not only beauty & nutritious food, it is aphrodisiac, promotes uplifting feeling & relaxation in body, heart & nerves. Happy food for your heart & brain!

# White Chocolate

Yields 2 cups of mixture
high power blender, chocolate mold and
thermometer needed

250 g finely grated cacao butter

100 g cashew nuts

100 g powdered sweetener (blended into powder

in the blender) such as coconut sugar

⅛ teaspoon salt

5 tablespoons lucuma powder

1. Place the cacao butter first in the blender followed by cashew nut, powdered sweetener and salt. (In case the cacao butter is very cold, warm over a double boiler and melt it only about 30 % of it).
2. Follow the "Serious Dark Chocolate" recipe process above. (Add lucuma powder instead of cacao powder.)

## FYI: Tempering

1. Cocoa butter fats are made up by different types of fatty acid molecules, which have different temperature to set. They have several different crystal structures of how each of fat molecule forms. By tempering-healing up & cooling down, it stabilize the crystallization of each fat so that it creates a beautiful, shiny, smooth mouth feel of chocolate.
2. I recommend using the powder sugar (dry sugar). When using the granule sugar such as coconut sugar, blend into powder in advance.
3. Make sure there is no water in the bowl.
4. Pay attention to the humidity. If the room is too humid, dry the air using air conditioner.

## Variation: Coloring Chocolate

1. Add the following into white chocolate for coloring!
2. Green: spirulina, green tea powder, moringa powder, green barley powder
3. Pink: beet powder, raspberry powder, strawberry powder
4. Yellow: turmeric powder, pumpkin powder
5. Brown: cacao powder
6. Purple: purple potato powder, blueberry powder, acai powder, maqui berry powder

# Almond Truffle

Rich, creamy, and smooth almond cream melts in your mouth.

Yields 12 pieces of 1 inch/2.5cm truffle                                              blender needed

⅔   cup (155g) almond butter
½   cup maple syrup or liquid sweetener of your choice
½   cup (110g) melted cacao butter
½   teaspoon vanilla extract                     ¼   teaspoon salt
5   tablespoons water                            6   tablespoons cacao powder

## Coating:
Cacao powder as required

1. Blend all ingredients in the blender except for cacao powder until smooth.
2. Add cacao powder and blend until well incorporated. (Do not overblend as it starts separate. You can also mix in a bowl.)
3. Transfer into a container and refrigerate for a few hours or until set.
4. Roll into 1 inch/2.5cm balls and place back into the fridge for a while to set the surface.
5. Roll in cacao powder when serving

> **FYI:** Just in case the mixture starts separate while blending, add another 1-2 tablespoons of water slowly while blending. It will help to fix it. Do not overblend after that.

# Arabian Orange Tahini Truffle

If you are serious tahini lover like I am, how can you miss out this treasure? Tahini + honey + orange… it's a winner!

Yields 12 pieces of 1 inch/2.5cm truffle                                              blender needed

⅔   cup (155g) tahini
½   cup (110g) melted cacao butter
100  ml (7 tablespoons) honey or liquid sweetener of your choice
1   tablespoon orange zest or a few drops orange essential oil
1   teaspoon vanilla extract                     ¼   teaspoon salt
5   tablespoons water                            4   tablespoons lucuma powder

## Coating:
Lucuma powder as required

1. Blend all ingredients in the blender except for lucuma powder until smooth.
2. Add lucuma powder and blend until well incorporated.
3. Transfer into a container and refrigerate for a few hours or until set.
4. Roll into 1 inch/2.5cm balls and place back into the fridge for a while to set the surface.
5. Roll in lucuma powder when serving.

# Hazelnut Fudge

Saltiness gives a nice kick to the fudge!

Yields 25 pieces of 1x1 inch/2.5x2.5cm fudge
Food processor and 5x5 inch/12.5x12.5cm container needed

- ¾ cup (105g) hazelnuts
- ¾ cup (90g) macadamia nuts
- ½ cup powdered coconut sugar (ground in the blender or grinder)
- 1 teaspoon vanilla extract
- ½ teaspoon hazelnut extract (optional)
- ¼ + ⅛ teaspoon salt
- ½ cup (120g) melted dark chocolate (see page 133 in this chapter)

1. Lightly grease the container with oil and cover with parchment paper or plastic wrap.
2. Process all ingredients except for the dark chocolate in the food processor until smooth.
3. Add dark chocolate and process until well incorporated.
4. Transfer into the container and refrigerate for a few hours or until set.
5. Take out from the container, cut into 1x1 inch/2.5x2.5cm cubes.


# Vanilla White Chocolate Fudge

Rich and creamy special treat!

Yields 25 pieces of 1x1 inch/2.5x2.5cm fudge
food processor and 5x5 inch/12.5x12.5cm container needed

- 1½ cups (180g) macadamia nuts
- ½ cup +2 tablespoons powdered coconut sugar (ground in the blender or grinder)
- 2 teaspoons vanilla extract
- ¼ teaspoon salt
- ½ cup (110g) melted cacao butter

1. Lightly grease the container with oil and cover with parchment paper or plastic wrap.
2. Process all ingredients except for the cacao butter in the food processor until smooth.
3. Add cacao butter and process until well incorporated.
4. Transfer into the container and refrigerate for a few hours or until set.
5. Take out from the container, cut into 1x1 inch/2.5x2.5cm cubes.

# Trico-Color Kisses: Lavender White/ Mint Green/ Rose Pink 3 color truffle

Those guys are just too good to be true, can't take my eyes off of you guys little babies!

Yields about 15 pieces of 1.4 inch/3.5cm kiss of each kind          blender needed

### Lavender white kiss:

1⅓  cups (175g) cashew nuts, soaked

⅓    cup (70g) cacao butter, melted and cooled down

½    cup honey or liquid sweetener of your choice

2     teaspoons vanilla extract

¼    teaspoons salt

1     teaspoon dried lavender

### Mint green kiss:

Using the same ingredients as lavender white kiss, replace dry lavender with the following:

½    teaspoon spirulina or green barley or any green powder

½    teaspoons peppermint extract or 2 drops mint essential oil or 1/4 cup mint leaves

### Rose pink kiss:

Using the same ingredients as lavender white kiss, replace dried lavender with the following:

6     pieces dried rose flowers

1-2  teaspoons beetroot juice or 2 teaspoons strawberry powder

### Coating:

½    cup (120g) melted dark chocolate (see page 133 in the Dark Chocolate in this chapter) for each kind

1. Blend all ingredients until smooth.
2. Transfer into the container and refrigerate for a few hours or until completely set.
3. Roll into 1.2 inch/3cm balls, place back into the fridge or freezer for a while to set the surface.
4. To cover with chocolate, prepare the nonstick sheet or parchment paper, a fork, and melted chocolate.
5. Dip 1 filling into the chocolate, scoop it out using a fork, drip off the excess chocolate gently and place onto the nonstick sheet or parchment paper, and then refrigerate until set.
6. In case the chocolate starts to get solid, warm it up in a double boiler or dehydrator.

# Snickers Bar

My pursuit for the "perfect caramel" has led to this equation, date + coconut + maple + lucuma = pretty yummy caramel-ly! But I realize I never eat the original :) ha ha! So I had to try it. Between us, I think it is much better than the original.

Yields 10 bars    need food processor, 4x8 inch/10x20cm container

## Vanilla cake:

1¾  cups (265g) ground almonds (see page 25 in the Techniques and Advance Preparation chapter for grinding)

2    tablespoons deseeded dates, finely chopped    1    teaspoon vanilla extract

4    tablespoons coconut oil, melted of solid    pinch salt

## Caramel:

1    cup (170g) deseeded dates, chopped and soaked in water (just enough to cover the dates) for 30 minutes

4    tablespoons coconut oil, melted if solid

2    tablespoons almond butter; if unavailable, use tahini or coconut butter

8    drops medicine flower's caramel flavor extract (optional)(see page 18 in the Staple Ingredients and Raw Alternatives chapter)

3    tablespoons maple syrup    2    tablespoons lucuma powder

1    teaspoon vanilla extract    ½    teaspoon salt

1    cup any nuts of your choice, chopped

## Coating:

1 cup (240g) melted dark chocolate (see page 133 in this chapter)

1. Lightly grease the container with oil and cover with parchment paper. (Both sides of the parchment paper should come out of the container so that it is easy to take the filling out.)

2. For the vanilla cake, process all the ingredients except for the coconut oil in the food processor, and then add coconut oil and process evenly. The consistency should be enough to be held together by hand, but still easy to break. If it is too dry, add a little more coconut oil.

3. Transfer into the container, press firmly, and keep in the freezer while making the caramel.

4. For the caramel, using the blender or food processor, blend all ingredients except for chopped nuts until smooth, transfer into a bowl and then fold in the nuts.

5. Pour the caramel onto the vanilla cake and flatten, then freeze for a few hours.

6. Take it out from the container and slice into 1 inch/2cm wide pieces, place back into the freezer.

7. To cover with chocolate, prepare the nonstick sheet or parchment paper, a fork, and melted chocolate.

8. Dip 1 bar into the chocolate, scoop it out using a fork, drip off the excess chocolate gently and place onto the nonstick sheet or parchment paper, and then refrigerate until set.

9. In case the chocolate starts to get solid, warm it up in a double boiler or dehydrator.

# SUPERFOOD BLISS BALLS AND CANDIES

These are literally a blissfully tasty little treat. Play with the ingredients and the flavour, the variations are infinite! Pack with loving energy into them and share with friends & family!

# Chocolate Bliss Ball

Yes! The simpler the best! We are blessed, each one of us!

Yields 15 pieces of 1.4 inch/3.5cm balls                                     food processor needed

| | |
|---|---|
| 2 | cups (240g) walnuts or pecan nuts |
| 1 | teaspoon vanilla extract |
| 1 | cup (170g) deseeded dates, chopped (adjust the quantity depending on softness of dates) |

| | |
|---|---|
| 4 | tablespoons cacao powder |
| ¼ | teaspoon salt |

## Coating:
Cacao powder as required

1. Process all the ingredients except for dates in the food processor into powder.
2. Add dates little by little while processing until evenly combined. The consistency should be enough to hold together by hand but not so wet. If it is too dry, add some more dates to process.
3. Roll the mixture into small balls and roll in cacao powder to serve.


# Apricot Chai Goji Ball

Coconuts, raisins, cashew nuts, cinnamon, and cardamom are the key elements for Indian flavor!

Yields 20 pieces of 1.4 inch/3.5cm balls                                     food processor needed

| | |
|---|---|
| 1 | cup (130g) cashew nuts |
| 1 | cup (75g) desiccated shredded coconut |
| 2 | teaspoon cinnamon powder |
| ½ | teaspoon cardamom powder |
| 1 | cup dates, deseeded and chopped (adjust the quantity depending on softness of dates) |
| 2 | tablespoons cacao nibs |

| | |
|---|---|
| ½ | cup sunflower seeds |
| ½ | teaspoon salt |
| 1 | cup (150g) dry apricots, chopped |
| 2 | tablespoons goji berries |

1. Process the first 6 ingredients in the food processor into rough chunks.
2. Add dates and apricots little by little while processing until evenly combined. The consistency should be enough to hold together by hand but not so wet. If it is too dry, add some more dates or apricots and process.
3. Transfer the mixture into a bowl and fold in all the rest of the ingredients.
4. Roll the mixture into small balls.

# Maca Caramel Candy

Yacon + lucuma + macadamia = super delicious caramel flavor!

Yields 15 pieces of 1.4 inch/3.5cm balls        food processor needed

2     cups (240g) macadamia nuts
2     tablespoons maca powder
1     tablespoons lucuma powder
1     teaspoon vanilla extract
5     drops medicine flower's caramel extract
      (optional) (see page 18 in the Staple
      Ingredients and Raw Alternatives chapter)
½    teaspoon salt
½    cup yacon syrup or molasses or maple
      syrup (for yacon, see page 49 for FYI on
      Homemade Nutella recipe in Sweet Creams
      and Sauces chapter)

## Coating:
Cacao nibs as required

Process all the ingredients except for yacon syrup in the food processor into puree. (See FYI below).

1. Add yacon syrup and process until evenly combined.
2. Transfer into a container and refrigerate for a few hours if it is too soft to roll.
3. Roll the mixture into small balls and roll in cacao nibs to serve.

**Variation: Chocolate-Covered Maca Caramel Candy**
Instead of coating with cacao nibs, dip in the chocolate!

Prepare ½ cup (120g) melted dark chocolate (see page 133 in Chocolates chapter). Dip 1 ball at a time into the chocolate, scoop it out using a fork, drip off the excess chocolate gently, place onto the nonstick sheet or parchment paper, and refrigerate until set.

> **FYI:** Macadamia nuts and Brazilian nuts are soft and oily compare to almonds, cashew nuts, or desicated coconuts. It will become "butter" when you keep processing. We want "buttery" smoothness for this candy while "crumbly" chunkiness for the other bliss ball for the texture.

# Brazilian Coffee Candy

Brazilian nuts are high in selenium, a great source of antioxidants. The coffee flavor perfectly compliments the rich and sweet Brazilian nuts and chocolate.

Yields 15 pieces of 1.4 inch/3.5cm balls                                    food processor needed

2     cups (260g) Brazilian nuts
3     tablespoons cacao powder
½     teaspoon vanilla extract
1     teaspoon coffee extract or 5 drops medicine flower's coffee extract (see page 18 in the Staple Ingredients and Raw Alternatives chapter)
½     teaspoon salt
1     cup (170g) deseeded dates, finely chopped (adjust quantity depending on softness of dates)

## Coating:
Cacao powder as required

1.  Process all the ingredients except for dates in the food processor into puree. (See page 147 for FYI on Maca Caramel Candy in this chapter)
2.  Add dates and process until evenly combined.
3.  Transfer into a container and refrigerate for a few hours if it is too soft to roll.
4.  Roll the mixture into small balls.
5.  Roll in cacao powder to coat.

### Variation: Chocolate-Covered Brazilian Coffee Candy
Instead of coating with cacao powder, dip in chocolate! (See page 147 for the variation of Maca Caramel Candy for the procedure.)

# Halva

Raw version of excess-sweet halva that I tried in Morocco! Rose, cinnamon and cardamom etc., … try many different flavors!

Yields 16 pieces of 1.2x1.2 inch/3x3cm cubes
5x5 inch/12x12cm container and food processor needed

2    cups (240g) white sesame seeds

½    cup powdered date sugar or coconut sugar (ground in the blender or grinder)

1    tablespoon orange zest or a few drops orange essential oil

¼    teaspoon salt

4    tablespoons (55g) melted cacao butter

4    tablespoons pistachio, roughly chopped

1. Lightly grease the container with oil and cover with parchment paper or plastic wrap.
2. Process all the ingredients except for melted cacao butter and pistachio in the food processor until just before the sesame seeds turn into a paste. (see FYI below)
3. Add melted cacao butter to process evenly.
4. Fold in the chopped pistachio.
5. Transfer into the container, press firmly, and refrigerate for a few hours to set.
6. Take out from the container and cut into 1.2x12 inch/3x3cm cubes.

**Variation: Chocolate-Coated Halva**
See page 147 for the variation of Maca Caramel Candy for the chocolate covering procedure.

**FYI:** If your food processor is not high powered enough to break down the sesame seeds into a paste, use a blender or grinder, then transfer into the food processor to continue the process.

# Chocolate-Covered Cherry Cake Pops

Be aware if there are kids around! These may disappear in a blink.

Yields 12 pieces
Food processor, lollipop sticks (or bamboo sticks) and foam block or flower oasis (optional)
needed

1    cup (120g) macadamia nuts

1    cup (130g) ashew nuts

6    tablespoons cacao powder

1    teaspoon vanilla extract

¼    teaspoon salt

½    cup (85g) deseeded dates, chopped (adjust the quantity depending on softness of dates)

½    cup (75g) dry cherries; if unavailable, use raisins and add a little cherry extract

## Coating:
1 cup (240g) melted dark chocolate (see page 133 in the Chocolates chapter)

## Topping:
Superfood of your choice such as acai powder, bee pollen, crunchy spirulina, cacao nibs

1.  Process the first 6 ingredients in the food processor into small chunks.
2.  Process all ingredients except for dates and cherries in the food processor into small chunks. (Do not overprocess, as macadamia nuts are easy to turn into butter)
3.  Add dates and cherries and process until evenly combined. The consistency should be enough to hold together by hand but not so wet. If it is too dry, add some more dates or cherries to process.
4.  Roll the mixture into small balls.
5.  Dip the end of a lollipop stick in the melted chocolate and push the end into the middle of the ball, then freeze it more than 30 minutes (that will help to keep it from falling apart while dipping into the chocolate.)
6.  Dip the pop into the melted chocolate, pick it up and drip off the chocolate gently and let it dry for a few moments.
7.  Place each pop into the foam block, decorate with the superfood of your choice, and then refrigerate until set.

> **FYI:** In case the chocolate starts to get solid, warm it up in a double boiler or dehydrator.

# ICE CREAM

It is too good and you might end up finishing it all before it is frozen—just like I often do. It's all right! You can call it pudding then :)

To make your ice cream more fun and yummy, serve with some nice crunchy toppings (see recipe on page 153) or you can just simply crumble leftover cookies and sweet crackers!

# Crunchy Topping for Ice Cream

Yields as much as you like :) food processor needed (optional)

Cacao nibs, nuts and seeds of your choice, dried fruits of your choice

1. Roughly process all the ingredients in the food processor until chunky. (You can also chop up with a knife.)

# Vanilla Ice Cream

My number-one favorite ice-cream flavor:) The simplest and the best!

Yields 3½ cups                                        blender needed

1½ cups (200g) cashew nuts, soaked

1¼ cups nut milk of your choice (see page 23 in the Techniques and Advance Preparation chapter)

½ cup honey or liquid sweetener of your choice

½ vanilla beans, scraped to use only seeds (optional)

2 teaspoons vanilla extract

⅛ teaspoon salt

2 tablespoons coconut oil, melted if solid

1 tablespoon lecithin

1. Blend all ingredients in the blender until smooth.
2. Add lecithin and coconut oil and blend until well incorporated.
3. Pour into ice-cream maker if you have one and follow the directions. If you don't have an ice-cream maker, pour into a container and freeze, stirring well a few times before completely frozen.

### Variation: Lavender Ice Cream
Add 2 teaspoons dried lavender flower and blend.

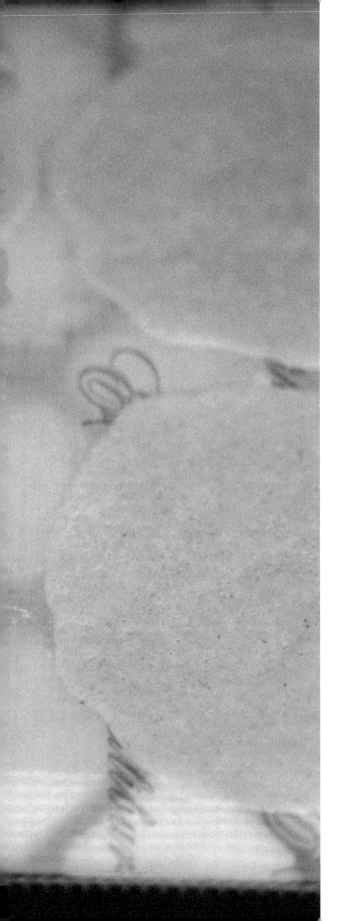

# Caramel
# Ice Cream Cone

To make ice cream much more fun and exciting!

Yields 8 pieces
blender and dehydrator needed

| | |
|---|---|
| 5 | tablespoons (40g) cashew nuts, soaked |
| 2 | tablespoons maple syrup |
| 2 | tablespoons lucuma powder |
| 1 | teaspoon vanilla extract |
| | pinch salt |
| ½ | cup water |
| | a few drops medicine flower's caramel extract (optional)(see page 18 in the Staple Ingredients and Raw Alternatives chapter) |
| 1 | tablespoon ground flaxseeds (see page 25 in the Techniques and Advance Preparation chapter for grinding) |

1. Blend all ingredients except for flaxseeds in the blender until smooth.
2. Add flaxseeds and blend until well incorporated.
3. Pour onto the nonstick sheet into 4 circles (on each sheet) and form into 5 inch/13cm diameter circles with offset spatula.
4. Dehydrate at 105-115 ° F/ 41-46 ° C for about 8 hours or until dry on top, then flip over. (If the other side is still wet, continue to dehydrate for a few hours until dry but still pliable.) When both sides are dry, cut the circles into halves.
5. Coning the middle point of the cutting line, roll into cone shapes, then fix the end by piercing with a toothpick.
6. Place the cones onto the mesh screen facing the coning edge on top, and continue to dehydrate until completely dry.

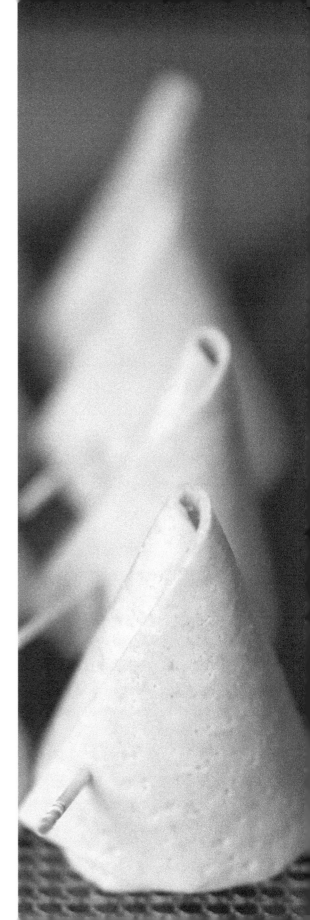

# Rum Raisin Ice Cream

Ho ho ho—this is another of my favorite flavors! Such an indulgence and luxury!

Yields 3½ cups                                          blender needed

1½   cups (200g) cashew nuts, soaked

1¼   cups nut milk of your choice (see page 23 in the Techniques and Advance Preparation chapter)

⅓    cup (6 tablespoons) coconut sugar syrup or liquid sweetener of your choice

1     teaspoon vanilla extract

1     teaspoon rum or 2-3 drops medicine flower's rum extract (see page 18 in the Staple Ingredients and Raw Alternatives chapter)

⅛    teaspoon salt

1     tablespoon lecithin

2     tablespoons coconut oil, melted if solid

6     tablespoons (55g) raisins

1. Blend all ingredients in the blender except for raisins until smooth.
2. Add raisins and blend only for a few seconds.
3. Pour into ice-cream maker if you have one and follow the directions. If you don't have an ice-cream maker, pour into a container and freeze, stirring well a few times before completely frozen.

### Variation: Green Tea Ice Cream
Omit rum, then add 2 tablespoons green tea powder and 2 more tablespoons liquid sweetener of your choice and blend.

### Green Tea Ice Cream Tiramisu
(See page 65 in the variation of green tea tiramisu in the Cakes, Doughnuts, and Crumbles chapter)

# Avocado Coconut Ice Cream

Smooth and creamy yet super light, summer tropical flavor! It is great with chunky tropical fruits on top!

Yields 4 cups                                                                      blender needed

2    cups nut milk of your choice (see page 23 in the Techniques and Advance Preparation chapter)

2    cups chopped avocado (about 1½-2 whole avocado)

½    cup honey or liquid sweetener of your choice

2    teaspoons lemon juice

1    teaspoon vanilla extract

     pinch salt

1    tablespoon lecithin

4    tablespoons coconut oil, melted if solid

4    tablespoons (45g) deseeded dates, chopped

1.  Blend all ingredients in the blender except for until smooth.
2.  Add dates and blend only for a few seconds.
3.  Pour into ice-cream maker if you have one and follow the directions. If you don' t have an ice-cream maker, pour into a container and freeze, stirring well a few times before completely frozen.

# Moringa Mint Chocolate Chip Ice Cream

These tiny little leaves of moringa are packed with tremendous nutrition and healing properties! The combination of mint and chocolate chips is an everlasting hit!

Yields 3½ cups                                                                blender needed

1½   cups (200g) cashew nuts, soaked
1¼   cups nut milk of your choice (see page 23 in the Techniques and Advance Preparation chapter)
½     cup honey or liquid sweetener of your choice
½-1 teaspoon peppermint extract or a few drops essential oil or ½ cup peppermint leaves
2      teaspoons moringa powder (see FYI below)
1      teaspoon vanilla extract
⅛     teaspoon salt
1      tablespoon lecithin
2      tablespoons coconut oil, melted if solid
½     cup (125g) roughly chopped dark chocolate (see page 133 of the Chocolates chapter)

1. Blend all ingredients in the blender except for dark chocolate until smooth.
2. Pour into ice-cream maker if you have one and follow the directions. If you don' t have an ice-cream maker, pour into the container and freeze, stirring well a few times before completely frozen.
3. Fold in dark chocolate before completely frozen.

FYI: The moringa leaves, called a "miracle herb," are packed with incredible nutrition. India' s ancient tradition of Ayurveda medicine says that, "Moringa leaves prevent 300 diseases."

# Quick Vanilla Sorbet

Here is my favorite easy and quick technique! Enjoy with chocolate ganache sauce (see page 49 of the Sweet Creams and Sauces chapter) or maca caramel sauce (see page 49 of the Sweet Creams and Sauces chapter) or crunchy toppings (see page 153 in this chapter)! Heaven it is.

Yields 3 cups
high power blender needed

¾    cup (100g) cashew nuts, soaked
3     cups + ⅓ cup nut milk of your choice (see page 23 in the Techniques and Advance Preparation chapter)
5–6 tablespoons honey or liquid sweetener of your choice
1     teaspoon vanilla extract
1     vanilla beans, scraped to use only seeds (optional)

1. Freeze the 3 cups of the nut milk in an ice cube tray overnight or until set. (⅓ cup nut milk is to keep to blend with other ingredients.)
2. Blend all ingredients (including the saved ⅓ cup nut milk) except for frozen nut milk in a high-power blender until smooth.
3. Add frozen nut milk and blend on high speed (use the tamper, if you are using Vitamix, to press the ice cubes toward the bottom while processing to facilitate easy blending) until all the ice is completely blended into the liquid and create the sorbet texture.
4. Transfer into a container and freeze for about 1 hour to set.

### Variations:
**Quick Lavender Sorbet:** Add 1 teaspoon dry lavender flower and blend.

**Quick Rum Raisin Sorbet:** Add 1 teaspoon rum or 1-3 drops medicine flower's rum extract (see page 18 in the Staple Ingredients and Raw Alternatives chapter) and blend, and then add 6 tablespoons raisins at the end and blend for a few seconds.

**Quick Green Tea Sorbet:** Add 2 tablespoons green tea powder and 1-2 more tablespoons sweetener and blend, and then add 6 tablespoons raisins at the end and blend for a few seconds.

**Quick Mint Chocolate Chip Sorbet:** Add ½ cup peppermint leaves or 1 teaspoon peppermint extract or a few drops essential oil (and 2 teaspoons any green powder) and blend, and then ½ cup (125g) roughly chopped dark chocolate at the end to fold in.

# Quick Peanut Butter Ice Cream

Who in the world does not like peanut butter and ice cream? The best-wanted combination here is!

Yields 3 cups                                              high powder blender needed

3      cups + ⅓ cup nut milk of your choice (see page 23 in the Techniques and Advance Preparation chapter)
⅓      cup (80g) peanut butter (or almond butter + 5-8 drops medicine flower's peanut extract: see page 18 in the Staple Ingredients and Raw Alternatives chapter)
5–6   tablespoons maple syrup or liquid sweetener of your choice
1      teaspoon vanilla extract

1. Freeze the 3 cups of nut milk in an ice cube tray overnight or until set. (⅓ cup nut milk is to keep to blend with other ingredients.)
2. Blend all ingredients (including the saved ⅓ cup nut milk) except for frozen nut milk in a high-power blender until smooth.
3. Add frozen nut milk and blend on high speed (use the tamper, if you are using Vitamix, to press the ice cubes toward the bottom while processing to facilitate easy blending) until all the ice is completely blended into the liquid and create the sorbet texture.
4. Transfer into a container and freeze for about 1 hour to set.

# Quick Orange Cacao Sorbet

Cacao and orange are the best of friends!

Yields 3¼ cups                                            high powder blender needed

½      cup (65g) cashew nuts, soaked
3      cups + ½ cup orange juice
5-6   tablespoons honey or liquid sweetener of your choice
1      teaspoon vanilla extract
2      tablespoons cacao powder
1      tablespoon orange zest or a few drops of orange essential oil

1. Freeze the 3 cups of orange juice in an ice cube tray overnight or until set. (1/2 cup orange juice is to keep to blend with other ingredients.)
2. Blend all ingredients (including the saved 1/2 cup orange juice) except for frozen orange juice in a high-power blender until smooth.
3. Add frozen orange juice and blend on high speed (use the tamper, if you are using Vitamix, to press the ice cubes toward the bottom while processing to facilitate easy blending) until all the ice is completely blended into the liquid and create the sorbet texture.
4. Transfer into a container and freeze for about 1 hour to set.

# Mini Banana Split

All-American super-easy-to-make banana split! I could eat it every day easily :)

Serves 1

½  banana, cut into half lengthwise

1-2  scoops ice cream of your choice (see any recipe of this chapter)

2-4  tablespoons vanilla whippy cream (see page 51 in the Sweet Creams and Sauces chapter)

1-2  teaspoons chocolate ganache sauce (see page 53 in the Sweet Creams and Sauces chapter)

1  fresh cherry; if unavailable, use other fruits

1. Place ice cream scoops on the chilled plate.
2. Place banana onto both sides of the ice cream.
3. Top with vanilla whippy cream, pour the chocolate ganache sauce, and then decorate with a cherry on top.

# Mango Blueberry Pops

Beautiful color layers make it a double delicious and fun pop! By the way, you can freeze any smoothie and make instant ice pops anytime!

Yields around 10-14 popsicles (vary depending on the popsicle size)
Bender and popsicle molds and sticks needed

2     cups chopped pineapple

1     cup chopped banana

1     cup chopped mango

1½   cups nut milk of your choice

1     tablespoon honey or liquid sweetener of your choice (optional)

1     cup blueberries

1. Blend all ingredients except for blueberries until smooth.
2. Pour the mixture into popsicle molds halfway.
3. Add blueberries to the rest of mixture and blend until smooth.
4. Gently pour over the first layer.
5. Set the sticks.
6. Freeze until set.

# THANKS!

Thanks to all my beautiful people!

Let's make lots of yummies and sweets to make us all happy and smile!